Keto Slow Cooker Cookbook

120+ Wholesome No-Fuss Meals for Busy People on a Budget. Enjoy Delicious and Healthy Low-Carb, Vegan and Vegetarian Recipes for Your Slow Cooker

Gabriel Greger

© **Copyright 2021 - Gabriel Greger - All rights reserved.**

The content contained within this book may not be reproduced, duplicated or transmitted without direct written permission from the author or the publisher.

Under no circumstances will any blame or legal responsibility be held against the publisher, or author, for any damages, reparation, or monetary loss due to the information contained within this book, either directly or indirectly.

Legal Notice:
This book is copyright protected. It is only for personal use. You cannot amend, distribute, sell, use, quote or paraphrase any part, or the content within this book, without the consent of the author or publisher.

Disclaimer Notice:
Please note the information contained within this document is for educational and entertainment purposes only. All effort has been executed to present accurate, up to date, reliable, complete information. No warranties of any kind are declared or implied. Readers acknowledge that the author is not engaged in the rendering of legal, financial, medical or professional advice. The content within this book has been derived from various sources. Please consult a licensed professional before attempting any techniques outlined in this book.

By reading this document, the reader agrees that under no circumstances is the author responsible for any losses, direct or indirect, that are incurred as a result of the use of the information contained within this document, including, but not limited to, errors, omissions, or inaccuracies.

Table of Contents

Introduction 1

Chapter 1 Slow-Cooker Easy Recipes 3

    Breakfast 3

    1. Slow-Cooker Breakfast Bake 3

        2. Slow-Cooker: Mexican Breakfast Casserole (Low-Carb) 4

    3. Keto Slow-Cooker Breakfast Casserole 5

    4. Slow-Cooker Egg and Sausage Breakfast Casserole 6

    5. Cheesy Waffle and Ham Breakfast Casserole 7

    6. Bourbon Buttermilk and Pie for Breakfast 8

    7. Healthy Low-Carb Breakfast with Sausage and Cheese (Gluten-Free) 9

    8. Paleo Breakfast Egg Muffins 10

    9. Slow-Cooker Keto Breakfast Sausage Casserole 11

Chapter 2 Lunch Recipes 12

    10. Slow-Cooker (Low-carb) Mexican-Lasagna Casserole 12

    11. Keto Slow-Cooker Garlic Chicken Recipe 13

    12. Pork Lettuce Wrap Meal 14

    13. Slow-Cooker Spaghetti Squash with Meatballs 14

    14. Fire-Roasted Tomato-Shrimp Tacos for Lunch 15

    15. Vinegar BBQ Chicken 16

    16. Spicy + Lime Chicken 16

    17. Slow-Cooker Coconut Quinoa Curry 17

Chapter 3 Dinner Recipes 18

    18. Slow-Cooker Sesame-Beef 18

    19. Slow-Cooker Pizza Chicken 18

    20. Crockpot Beef-Short-Ribs with Creamy Mushroom-Sauce (Low-carb, Keto) 19

    21. Slow-Cooker Italian-Beef 20

22. (Keto) Slow-Cooker Tri-Tip 21

23. Slow-Cooker (Keto) Meatball-Casserole 22

24. (Low-carb) Slow-Cooker Butter-Chicken 23

25. Low-Carb Mushroom Lover's Pot Roast Slow-Cooker 24

26. Green Chile Beef Shredded Cabbage Bowl with Avocado Salsa 25

Chapter 4 Dessert Recipes 26

27. Slow-Cooker Low-carb Pumpkin Cake 26

28. Slow-Cooker Low-carb Mint Chocolate Cake 27

29. Slow-Cooker Dark Chocolate Cake 28

30. Slow-Cooker Low-Carb Chocolate Lava Cake 29

31. Crockpot Sugar-Free Dairy-Free Fudge 30

32. Slow-Cooker Keto Maple Custard 30

33. Easy Slow-Cooker Lemon Custard 31

34. Crockpot Sugar-Free Pumpkin Pie Bars 32

35. Crockpot Blueberry Lemon Custard Cake 33

36. Slow-Cooker Raspberry Cream Cheese Coffee Cake 34

Chapter Five Vegetable recipes 35

37. Slow-Cooker Eggplant Parmesan (Breakfast) 35

38. Slow-Cooker Mac and Cheese (breakfast) 36

39. Eggs Over Cauliflower Hash (Breakfast) 37

40. Slow-Cooker Butternut Squash Dal (Lunch) 38

41. Slow-Cooker Cheesy Butternut Squash Macaroni (Lunch) 39

42. Super Easy Skinny Veggie Crockpot Lasagna (Lunch) 40

43. Vegetarian Lentil Tortilla Soup (Dinner) 41

44. Slow-Cooker Enchilada Quinoa Bake (Dinner) 42

45. Slow-Cooker Vegetarian Chili Mac (Dinner) 43

46. Quinoa Black Bean Crockpot Stuffed Peppers (Dinner) 44

Chapter Six Vegan Recipes 45

- 47. Slow-Cooker Vegan Chili (Breakfast) 45
- 48. Slow-Cooker Breakfast Beans (Breakfast) 46
- 49. Ratatouille with Lentils (Breakfast) 46
- 50. Fruit Compote with Ginger (Lunch) 47
- 51. Slow-Cooked Sweet and Sour Cabbage (Lunch) 47
- 52. Slow-Cooker Burrito Bowls (Lunch) 48
- 53. Carrot Rillettes with Dukkah (Dinner) 49
- 54. Vegan Jambalaya Slow-Cooker (Dinner) 50
- 55. Slow-Cooker Moroccan Chickpea Stew (Dinner) 51
- 56. Vegan Keto Walnut Chili (Dinner) 52

Chapter Seven Fish and Seafood 53

- 57. Slow-Cooker Fish and Tomatoes (Low-Carb, Paleo, Whole30) 53
- 58. Slow-Cooker Fish Fillets 54
- 59. Keto Slow-Cooker Tilapia 55
- 60. Slow-Cooker Seafood Stew Recipe 55
- 61. Seafood Cioppino 56
- 62. Slow-Cooker Shrimp Boil 57
- 63. Crockpot New Orleans Spicy Barbecue Shrimp Recipe 58
- 64. Slow-Cooker Maple Salmon 59
- 65. Slow-Cooker Cajun Corn and Shrimp Chowder 59
- 66. Low Cooker/Instant Pot Coconut Curry Shrimp (Low-Carb, Paleo, Whole30) 60
- 67. Crockpot Shrimp and Grits Recipe 60
- 68. Crockpot Low Country Boil 61
- 69. Slow-Cooker Fish Au Gratin 62
- 70. Low-Cooker Tuna Noodle Casserole 63
- 71. Crock-Pot Crab Rangoon Dip Recipe 64

Chapter Eight Soup and Stew Recipes 65

    72. Slow-Cooker Low-carb Zuppa Toscana Soup 65

    73. Garden Tomato Soup 66

    74. Slow-Cooker Curried Butternut Squash Soup 67

    75. Crock-Pot Chicken Soup (Low-Carb + Keto) 67

    76. Slow-Cooker Vegetable Soup 68

    77. Slow-Cooker Mediterranean Stew 69

    78. Slow-Cooker Vegetable and Tofu Thai Stew 70

    79. Slow-Cooker Vegetable Stew 71

    80. Southwestern Sweet Potato Stew 72

    81. Low-Carb Beef Cabbage Stew 73

Chapter Nine Rice Recipes 74

    82. Keto Crockpot Jambalaya 74

    83. Crockpot Cauliflower Fried Rice 75

    84. Coconut Curry Chicken with Cauliflower Rice (Keto, low-carb) 76

    85. Keto Chicken Gumbo 77

    86. Low-carb Vegan Rice and Beans 78

    87. Crockpot Rice Pudding 79

    88. Salsa Chicken Cauliflower Rice Bowls 80

    89. Keto Chicken and Cauliflower Rice Soup 81

    90. Slow-Cooker Keto Turkey Kale Rice Soup 82

    91. Crockpot Luau Pork with Cauli Rice 83

    92. Crock-Pot Asian Beef and Paleo 'Rice' Bowls 84

    93. Slow-Cooker Chicken and Rice Soup 85

Chapter Ten Side Recipes 86

    94. Slow-Cooker Three Cheese Spaghetti Squash 86

    95. Slow-Cooker Pepper Jack Cauliflower 87

96. Slow-Cooker Lemon-Garlic Asparagus (Low-Carb, Paleo, Whole30) 88

97. Crockpot Buttered Garlic Mushrooms 88

98. Crockpot Loaded Cauliflower Casserole 89

99. Slow-Cooker Ratatouille 89

100. Slow-Cooker Low-Carb Santa Fe Chicken 90

101. Crockpot Chicken Fajitas 91

102. Slow-Cooker Cabbage and Onions 92

103. Crock-Pot Zucchini and Yellow Squash 92

104. Slow-Cooker Mongolian Beef 93

105. Slow-Cooker Crack Chicken 94

106. No-Hassle Crockpot Keto Meatloaf 95

107. Slow-Cooker Low-Carb Meatloaf Wrapped in Bacon 96

108. Keto Slow-Cooker Buffalo Chicken 97

Chapter Eleven Beef 98

109. Chipotle Beef Barbacoa Recipe (Slow-Cooker/Crockpot) 98

110. Instant Pot (or Slow-Cooker) Low-Carb Southwestern Beef Stew 99

111. Low-carb Beef Stroganoff 100

112. Slow-Cooker Low-carb Meatloaf Recipe 101

113. Barbecue Meatloaf Slow-Cooker 102

114. Perfectly Simple and Sliceable Crockpot Roast Beef 103

115. Healthified Moroccan Beef 103

Chapter Twelve Chicken 104

116. Slow-Cooker Mandarin Chicken – Low-Carb and Gluten-Free 104

117. Crock-Pot Slow-Cooker Crack Chicken 105

118. Low-carb Spicy Chicken 106

119. Slow-Cooker Low-carb Sesame Ginger Chicken 107

120. Low-carb BBQ Chicken in the Slow-Cooker 108

121. Crockpot Pepper Chicken (Slow-Cooker) 109

122. Creamy Chicken with Bacon and Cheese Slow-Cooker (Low-Carb and Keto) 110

123. Slow-Cooker Chicken Caprese Casserole (Low-Carb, Keto) 111

Chapter Thirteen Pork 112

124. Crockpot Cola Pulled Pork (Low-carb) 112

125. Keto Slow-Cooker Pulled Pork 113

126. Low-carb Pork Chops in Crockpot With Spice Rub (Recipe) 114

127. Low-carb Slow-Cooker Spicy Pulled Pork 115

128. Keto Slow-Cooker Pork Roast 116

129. Keto Cuban Pork (Lechón) 117

Conclusion 118

Introduction

The keto diet is a low-carbohydrate, high-fat diet that offers many health benefits. It has been proven over time that such a diet helps you to improve your health, and you end up losing weight. Keto diets may also benefit people who have asthma, obesity, schizophrenia, and Alzheimer's disease. The word "ketogenic" is a low-carb diet. The concept is for people to eat less carbohydrate and more fat and protein. You eliminate carbohydrates, such as pastries and white bread. It requires a dramatic decrease in the consumption of carbohydrates and its substitution with fat. You will do it easily if you consume fewer than 50g of carbohydrates a day; your body gradually runs out of food (blood sugar). Typically, this will take 3 to 4 days. You will then continue breaking down protein and fat for energy, which will lead you to lose weight. While on a keto diet, you eat far fewer carbohydrates, you maintain moderate protein intake, and increase your fat intake. Reducing carbohydrates consumption puts the body in a stable condition called ketosis, where fat is consumed so the energy can be utilized and be received from the food to the muscles.

But people have heard many times in their lives how damaging the fat is to their wellbeing, especially the waistline. They were told to stop it and to prefer diets that are rich in carbs and lean proteins instead. Generally, this seems like useful guidance. We have followed this guide to the extent that we are a progressively obese world and challenged by chronic health problems induced, in part, by our fat avoidance at all costs. Therefore, we do better when we know better. You set out to find more about how you can create significant improvements when you see an issue that happens in your fitness and the way you think about yourself. There is a probability that you have tried on low-fat diets at some stage, and you find yourself discouraged and disappointed. Now is the opportunity to read more—and to know something because you can perform better—and with the ketogenic diet, everything can be achieved.

We also know from scientific proof that so many carbohydrates, including nutritious ones, will trigger an unhealthy increase in blood sugar levels, which may contribute to severe inflammatory disorders, like cardiac disease and diabetes. We now know that individuals who adopt long-term low-carbohydrate diets experience less of these health problems and have improved outcomes while reducing pounds, whereas keeping a balanced diet. Low-carbohydrate people are not just slimmer.

They are often healthier. What we all also realize is that there is an improvement to the low-carb diets of past years, and whenever we talk of the ketogenic diet, it is the change that we are referring to.

When you have a diet schedule that you can sustain without getting dissatisfied and one in which you can potentially produce success, there is just one hurdle remaining in your path: you are too exhausted to make special visits to the food store to spend hours in the kitchen doing extra work and spend hours a day planning meals. There are not enough individuals who have the capacity for this. And when you eat ketogenically, it can also be challenging to either take something and then go or make a quick meal that you're not dissatisfied with. The solution to these issues is to stay calmly in your kitchen. It's the Slow-Cooker.

The ketogenic diet can base out of various menus like the low in carbs; people who practice a vegan lifestyle can also benefit from keto recipes. Now, Slow-Cookers and keto lifestyles can have these categories in common. As people who want low-carb, vegan meals but want to preserve the food nutrients, even more, will have to use a Slow-Cooker; hence Slow-Cookers can be the star of the show when preparing low-keto-carb, full of nutritious recipes.

For decades, the home's favorite has been the Slow-Cooker. But, sometimes, we started to leave other cooking techniques down the fine, and this silent little appliance was moved to the back of the closet. Ok, now is the time for your Slow-Cooker to breathe fresh life into it. In this book, every meal and side dish comes with fewer grams of net carbohydrates, ensuring they suit your ketogenic lifestyle perfectly. Go into the kitchen and pull your Slow-Cooker out. Dust it off and plan to eat some of the most amazing ketogenic meals you've ever had.

Chapter 1
Slow-Cooker Easy Recipes

Breakfast

1. Slow-Cooker Breakfast Bake

Servings: 12 / **Prep. Time:** 15 min. / **Cook Time:** 2 hrs.

Ingredients:

- 2 lbs. of ground sausage
- 4 cups of cheddar cheese
- 12 large eggs
- ½ cup of sweet red pepper chopped
- ½ cup of chopped onion
- 1 tsp. of salt
- ½ cup of heavy cream
- ½ tsp. of black pepper freshly ground
- 1 bacon package

Instructions:

1. Cook the bacon in a skillet, then set aside.
2. Sizzle red peppers and onions for about 3 minutes, using the same pan with bacon grease. Then add sausage and vegetables previously chopped into the skillet.
3. Mix heavy cream, eggs, pepper, and salt in a wide cup. Scramble until smooth.
4. Put sausage mixture onto the bottom of a Slow-Cooker.
5. Add 2 cups of cheese on top.
6. Add bacon on top.
7. Then top with a mixture of eggs. Then again top with two cups of cheese.
8. On high heat, cook for 2 hours at least, or till 160°F.
9. Serve.

Net Carbs: 2g / **Calories:** 518 / **Fat:** 40g / **Carbs:** 2g / **Protein:** 34g / **Fiber:** 0g

2. Slow-Cooker: Mexican Breakfast Casserole (Low-Carb)

Servings: 10 / **Prep. Time:** 15 min. / **Cook Time:** 5 hrs.

Ingredients:

- 12 ounces of ground pork
- ½ tsp. of garlic powder
- ½ tsp. of coriander
- 1 tsp. of cumin
- 1 tsp. of chili powder
- ¼ tsp. of salt
- ¼ teaspoon pepper
- 1 cup of salsa
- 10 eggs
- 1 cup of heavy cream
- 1 cup of pepper jack cheese
- You can add sour cream, avocado salsa, cilantro for additional toppings

Instructions:

1. Cook the pork sausage in a large skillet over medium heat until it is no longer pink.
2. Add salsa and seasonings. Put aside to cool off slowly.
3. Whisk the cream and egg in another bowl.
4. Add to eggs the pork, add the cheese, and blend.
5. Grease the crockpot bottom and pour it into the mixture.
6. Cover and cook for 2 1/2 hours or 5 hours on low heat.

Net Carbs: 2g / **Calories:** 284 / **Fats:** 23g / **Protein:** 15g / **Fiber:** 1g / **Sugar:** 1g

3. Keto Slow-Cooker Breakfast Casserole

Servings: 10 / **Prep. Time:** 15 min. / **Cook Time:** 1hr. 45min.

Ingredients:

- 6 large eggs
- 3 large bacon slices
- 3 tbsp. of chopped shallots
- ½ cup of chopped red bell pepper
- 1 cup of chopped white mushrooms
- 8 large leaves of kale shredded finely
- 1 tbsp. of butter or ghee
- 1 cup of shredded Parmesan cheese
- Salt and pepper, to taste

Instructions:

1. From the kale, strip the stems and cut into small pieces.
2. Fry the bacon and add the red pepper, mushroom, and shallot. Sauté until softened.
3. Add the kale and turn off the heat to wilt but not cook the kale.
4. Beat the eggs until well mixed with salt and pepper.
5. Turn on the Slow-Cooker and bring the butter to melt. Brush the interior of the Slow-Cooker with the melted butter. Put the sautéed vegetables into the Slow-Cooker foundation.
6. Scatter the cheese over the vegetables and pour over the egg mixture.
7. Whisk over and cook for about 1.5 hrs. or on less heat for 6 hrs. These times will wildly vary based on your Slow-Cooker.

Net Carbs: 4g / **Cal:** 313 / **Protein:** 23.1g / **Fat:** 22.2g / **Fiber:** 2.1g / **Sugars:** 2.7g

4. Slow-Cooker Egg and Sausage Breakfast Casserole

Servings: 6–8 / **Prep. Time:** 10 min. / **Cook Time:** 3hrs.

Ingredients:

- 1 medium broccoli, chopped
- 12- oz. of sliced and cooked dairy farm little links
- 1 cup of divided of shredded cheddar
- 10 eggs
- ¾ cup of whipping cream
- 2 minced garlic cloves
- ½ tsp. of salt
- ¼ tsp. of pepper

Instructions:

1. Grease well the Slow-Cooker (6 quarts).
2. Layer half the broccoli, half the sausage, and half the cheese in the Slow-Cooker. Repeat with broccoli, bacon, and cheese leftover.
3. Whisk eggs, garlic, whipping cream, salt, and pepper in a wide bowl until well mixed. Pour over ingredients that are layered.
4. Cover and cook on low heat for 4 to 5 hours or 2 to 3 hours on high, until browned on the edges.

Net Carbs: 5.3g / **Cal:** 484 / **Protein:** 26.13g / **Carbohydrates:** 5.39g / **Fiber:** 1.18g

5. Cheesy Waffle and Ham Breakfast Casserole

Servings: 4 / **Prep. Time**: 5 min. / **Cook Time**: 50min.

Ingredients:

- 125g (4.4oz.) of leftover ham(cubed)
- 6 large eggs
- 500 ml. (2 cups) of whole milk
- ½ tsp. of paprika
- 1tsp. of salt
- 226g (8oz.) of extra mature cheddar cheese (grated)
- 300g (10.5oz.) of cut waffles in cubes

Instructions:

1. To 180°C–190°C/350°F, preheat the oven.
2. In a large bowl, combine milk, eggs, paprika, and salt.
3. In a large skillet, add half a layer of waffles, half a ham, and half a grated cheese. Then repeat with half of the waffles, ham, and cheese left.
4. Pour into the skillet the egg mixture.
5. Cover and bake 30 minutes in a preheated oven.
6. Remove the skillet and put away the foil. Return to the oven, then continue cooking for another 20 to 30 minutes...

Net Carbs: 37g / **Cal**: 683 / **Fat:** 42g / **Saturated Fat:** 20g / **Protein:** 38g / **Sugar:** 8g

6. Bourbon Buttermilk and Pie for Breakfast

Servings: 12 / **Prep. Time**: 10min. / **Cook Time:** 45min.

Ingredients:

- 1 (unbaked) piecrust 9-inch
- 3 large eggs
- 1 ¼ cup (160g) of granulated sugar
- 3 tbsp. of all-purpose flour
- ¼ tsp. of kosher salt
- ½ cup (113g) of unsalted butter (cooled and melted)
- 3/4 cup (180ml) of buttermilk
- 3 tbsp. of bourbon
- 1 tsp. of lemon zest
- 1 tbsp. lemon juice
- 1 tsp. of vanilla extract
- 1/8 tsp. of freshly grated nutmeg
- Optional: whipped cream for serving

Instructions:

1. To 350°F/176°C, preheat the oven.
2. Prepare your pie crust.
3. Move pie crust to a 9-inch pie plate, trim the sides, fold over the side of the pan and crimp the sides with your fingertips or a fork around the pie plate and refrigerate when making the fill.
4. Whisk eggs and sugar together in a big bowl until frothy. Add left ingredients, then whisk till smooth.
5. In cold baked pie crust, pour filling.
6. Bake 35–45 minutes in the oven or until almost finished. After 15 minutes in the oven, be sure to cover the corners of the pie crust with the aluminum foil.
7. Upon finished, remove it then let cool on a cooling rack for at least two hours until serving.

Optional: cover each slice before serving with a spoonful of whipped cream.

Net Carbs: 30g / **Cal:** 255 / **Fat:** 13g / **Saturated Fat:** 7g / **Protein:** 3g / **Sugar:** 22g

7. Healthy Low-Carb Breakfast with Sausage and Cheese (Gluten-Free)

Servings: 9 / **Prep. Time:** 5min. / **Cook Time:** 40min.

Ingredients:

- 1 lb. of breakfast sausage
- 6 cloves of garlic (minced)
- 12 large egg
- ½ cup of heavy cream
- 2 cups (divided) of cheddar cheese
- 2 tbsp. of (chopped) of fresh parsley
- ¼ tsp. of sea salt
- ¼ tsp. of black pepper
- 3 cups of broccoli

Instructions:

1. Cook the hazelnut garlic in the skillet over medium heat for about a minute, until it is brown.
2. Cook the eggs for about 10 minutes until browned, removing with a spatula.
3. Preheat the oven to 400°F in the meantime.
4. Defrost them in boil water for about 5–7 minutes when using broccoli until crisp. Then in an ice bath, plunge it to stop cooking, rinse and pat dry.
5. Whisk the heavy cream, egg, cheddar cheese (half), parsley, black pepper, and sea salt together in a large bowl.
6. Grease the ceramic or glass-bottom 8x8 in the casserole dish. The crumbled sausage is arranged uniformly at the lower part of the casserole platter.
7. Pour over the sausage the egg mixture. Sprinkle the leftover cheddar cheese.
8. Bake until the eggs are cooked, and the cheese melted for about 30 mins.

Net Carbs: 1g / **Cal:** 281 / **Protein:** 17g

8. Paleo Breakfast Egg Muffins

Servings: 12 / **Prep. Time:** 10min. / **Cook Time:** 45min.

Ingredients:

- 1 cup of broccoli
- 1 cup of cauliflower
- 1 cup of red bell pepper
- 2 minced cloves of garlic
- 2 tablespoon of olive oil
- 8 large egg
- ¼ cup of coconut cream
- 1 teaspoon of sea salt
- ½ teaspoon of black pepper

Instructions:

1. The oven is preheated to 400°F (204°C). Cover a baking dish with foil or parchment paper (grease when using foil).
2. Toss broccoli, cabbage, red pepper, garlic powder, and olive oil together in a large bowl.
3. Place vegetables on the baking sheet in a single layer. Roast for 15–20 minutes in the preheated oven, until broccoli edges are browned.
4. Meanwhile, cover 12 cups of muffins with muffin liners, or use a silicone one.
5. Leave the oven on until the vegetables are cooked. Equally, place the vegetables in muffin cups.
6. The eggs, coconut milk, sea salt, and black pepper are whisked together. The egg mixture is poured over the vegetables into the muffin cups.
7. Bake until the eggs are ready for 15–20min.

Net Carbs: 1g / **Cal:** 94 / **Protein:** 5g / **Fat:** 7g / **Total Carbs**: 2g / **Fiber:** 1g / **Sugar:** 1g

9. Slow-Cooker Keto Breakfast Sausage Casserole

Servings: 6 / **Prep. Time:** 10 min. / **Cook Time:** 3hrs. 10min.

Ingredients:

- 1 lb. of pork sausage
- 1 tsp. of dry-rubbed sage
- 1 tsp. of dried thyme
- ½ tsp. of ground black pepper
- ½ tsp. of salt
- ½ cup of chopped red onion
- ½ tsp. of garlic powder
- ½ cup of chopped green bell pepper
- ½ cup of chopped red bell pepper
- 1 tsp. of ghee
- 12 large eggs
- ½ cup of coconut milk
- 1 tsp. of nutritional yeast

Instructions:

1. Heat a medium cast-iron skillet for 2 minutes over medium heat. Add the pork sausage in crumbles. Cook for three mins.
2. Stir in the thyme, sage, powdered garlic, sea salt, and black pepper. Cook 5 more minutes, then turn off. Stir in the bell peppers and the chopped onion.
3. Grease the Slow-Cooker bowl with ghee. Pour the vegetable mixture and pork into the Slow-Cooker. Whisk the eggs, nutritional yeast, and coconut milk in a large mixing bowl until the eggs are thoroughly mixed. Pour it now over the pork mixture in the Slow-Cooker.
4. Cover and cook for 2 to 3 hours at low heat until the eggs are completely cooked.
5. Serve hot.

Net Carbs: 5g / **Fats:** 37g / **Protein:** 27g

Chapter 2
Lunch Recipes

10. Slow-Cooker (Low-carb) Mexican-Lasagna Casserole

Servings: 10 / **Prep. Time:** 20min. / **Cook Time:** 2hr. 30min.

Ingredients:

- 1 tablespoon of olive oil
- 2 lbs. of lean ground beef
- 1 small onion (chopped)
- 1 tbs. of Kalyn's taco seasoning
- 1 cup of pace Picante sauce
- 2 cans (10oz.) of rotel tomatoes and green chilies
- 6 low-carb tortillas (cut into half)
- 2 cups of cottage cheese
- 1 can (4oz.) of diced green chiles (drained),
- 2 eggs
- 3 cups of grated Mexican cheese blend

Instructions:

1. In a big, heavy frying pan, heat the oil, add in the ground beef, split it apart using your fingers, and cook on medium-high heat until the beef is golden brown and cooked thru. Pull the beef away using a turner or an old school potato masher as it cooks in little bits.
2. Move it over to the side when the beef is finished, add a little more oil if appropriate, and cook the onion (diced) for a couple of mins., then mix the onion with beef.
3. Add Kalyn's Taco Sauce, Ro-Tel tomatoes, and salsa and cook at low heat until much of the liquid is evaporated, and you don't see any liquid as you draw a turner over the bottom of the skillet.
4. Mix in the cottage cheese, washed green chilies, a cup of cheese, and eggs while the beef mixture is heating.
5. Break the tortillas in half with kitchen shears and spread some oil with a non-stick brush on the Slow-Cooker.
6. Create a layer of tortillas in the crockery casserole dish frame, utilizing the tortillas cut side to go around the straight edges. Using as few of the tortillas as you may cover the rim.

7. Create a base of half the mixture of spicy beef, half the mixture of cottage cheese, and a cup of grated cheese (or more). Then render the tortillas, cottage cheese, mixture meat mixture, and grated cheese a second layer each.
8. Close the Slow-Cooker and cook over high for around 2 ½hrs. until the saucepan bursts, and the cheese is melted perfectly.
9. If you are cooking in a casserole crack, you can brown a dish in a 200°C/400°F oven for almost 15min if appropriate.

Calories: 466 / **Fat:** 25g / **Cholesterol**: 157mg / **Sodium:** 711mg / **Net Carb**: 10g / **Fiber:** 3g / **Sugar:** 6g / **Protein:** 45g

11. Keto Slow-Cooker Garlic Chicken Recipe

Servings: 4 / **Prep. Time:** 5min. / **Cook Time:** 8hrs.

Ingredients:

- 1 tbsp. of (15ml) of olive oil
- 4 (600g) chicken thighs (with skin on)
- 1 garlic head
- 1 ½ cup (360ml) of chicken broth, warm
- Salt and freshly ground black pepper
- Chives, for garnish.

Instructions:

1. In a skillet, heat the oil and brown that chicken skin-side until crispy and golden.
2. Meanwhile, peel off the cloves from the garlic head. Halve each and add to Slow-Cooker before dumping in the heated chicken broth. When the bits of chicken have caramelized on the skin-side, utilize tongs to remove them from the skillet to the Slow-Cooker, skin-side up. Cook heavily for 3 hrs.
3. Remove chicken then season with fresh grounded black pepper salt. Decorate with chives.

Calories: 241 / **Net Carb:** 1g / **Protein:** 16g / **Fats:** 18g / **Sugar:** 0g / **Fiber:** 0g

12. Pork Lettuce Wrap Meal

Servings: 3 / **Prep. Time:** 15min. / **Cook Time:** 6hrs.

Ingredients:

- 1 pound of boneless pork shoulder
- ¼ teaspoon of salt
- ¼ teaspoon of pepper
- 1 tablespoon of favorite spice seasoning
- 1 medium yellow onion (chopped)
- ¼ teaspoon of garlic powder
- 1 cup of chicken broth

Instructions:

1. Mix all the ingredients in a Slow-Cooker, which is 5-quarters or greater.
2. Cover it and cook for 6 hrs. on high.
3. Let it cool down, then shred it using a fork.
4. Keep the shredded pork for up to a week in the refrigerator.
5. Serve it with buttered lettuce leaves, mustard, tomato, and toppings of your choice.

Calories: 363 / **Net Carb:** 2.5g / **Protein:** 28g / **Fats:** 24g / **Fiber:** 1g

13. Slow-Cooker Spaghetti Squash with Meatballs

Servings: 4 / **Prep. Time:** 15min. / **Cook Time:** 4hrs.

Ingredients: Calories: 235/**Net Carb:** 9.8g/**Protein:** 15g/**Fats:** 13g/**Sodium:** 504mg /**Fiber:** 2g

- 1 medium spaghetti squash
- 1 ½ cups of crushed tomatoes
- ½ teaspoon salt
- ½ teaspoon of garlic powder
- ¼ teaspoon of pepper
- ¼ teaspoon of dried oregano
- 16 chicken meatballs (gluten-free)
- 2 tablespoon of butter/olive oil
- Additional pepper and salt to taste

Instructions

1. Cut the squash spaghetti in half (crosswise). Place it beneath the Slow-Cooker (cut-side down).
2. Mix the tomatoes, garlic powder, salt, pepper, and oregano in a processor/blender. Puree until smooth. Pour onto the Slow-Cooker's bottom.
3. Place the meatballs over the tomatoes, and the spaghetti squash around them. Cook for 6–7hrs. on low, or 3 to 4hrs. on high. Remove the spaghetti squash from the Slow-Cooker, utilizing tongs and kitchen gloves. Drive seeds out and dispose of. To eliminate moisture, scoop out the flesh to a sieve/colander and let it soak for a few minutes. Move to a bowl and apply butter/olive oil to throw. Divide into 4 plates, then finish the topping with meatballs and sauce.

14. Fire-Roasted Tomato-Shrimp Tacos for Lunch

Servings: 5 / **Prep. Time:** 10min. / **Cook Time:** 1hr. 55min.

Ingredients:

- 1 lb. of Medium shrimp (should be peeled and tails off and would be fresh or frozen and then thawed)
- 1 tablespoon of olive oil (or avocado oil)
- ½ cup of chopped onion
- 14.5oz. can of fire-roasted stewed tomatoes
- ½ cup of chunky salsa
- 1 (about ½–2/3 cup) of bell pepper (chopped),
- Dash of Sea salt and Black pepper
- ½ teaspoon of cumin
- ½ teaspoon of chili powder/ancho chili powder
- ¼ teaspoon of paprika/cayenne pepper
- 1 teaspoon of minced garlic
- 3–4 tablespoon of chopped cilantro (2–3 tablespoon for plating)
- Tortillas to serve

Instructions:

1. Make sure that the shrimp are peeled first and that the tails are off. If you use frozen shrimp, thaw quickly for 10min., then peel.
2. Layer the bottom of the pot with your fresh shrimp. Sprinkle with 1 tablespoon of olive oil. Mix the minced onion in, too.
3. Drain the roasted tomatoes from the canned and then pour them over the shrimp. Stir them.
4. Add your bell pepper and the majority of the products; this includes your cilantro and seasonings. Stir them together.
5. Place (crockpot) Slow-Cooker on low for 2–3hrs. Or high for 90min–2hrs.
6. Check on the shrimp for around 1 hr of cooking high. Put on medium heat for the next 30min. to an hour if they look almost finished. They should be nicely seasoned and pink, close to that of steamed shrimp.
7. Serve with sliced cabbage, salad, rice, avocado with gluten-free corn, paleo tortillas!
8. Cover with jalapeno and gluten-free flour tortillas and with more cilantro.

Calories: 115 / **Net Carb:** 3g / **Protein:** 14g / **Fats:** 3g / **Sugar:** 2g / **Fiber:** 2g

15. Vinegar BBQ Chicken

Servings: 6 / **Prep. Time:** 10min. / **Cook Time:** 4hr.

Ingredients:

- 2 cups of water
- 1 cup of white vinegar
- ¼ cup of sugar
- 1 tbsp. of reduced-sodium chicken base
- 1 tsp. of red pepper flakes (crushed)
- ¾ tsp. of salt
- 1 ½ pound of (boneless, skinless) chicken breasts

Instructions:

1. Mix the first six supplies into a small bowl. Holding the chicken in a 3-qt. Slow-Cooker; add a blend of vinegar. Cook (covered) for 4–5 hrs. or until the chicken is soft.
2. Remove the chicken; cool slightly. Reserve 1 cup of cooking juices; remove all leftover juices. Shred chicken using two forks. Return meat and those reserved cooking juices to Slow-Cooker, heat through.
3. Serve chicken mixture on buns if needed.

Calories: 134 / **Net Carb:** 2g / **Protein:** 23g / **Fats:** 3g / **Sugar:** 3g / **Fiber:** 0g

16. Spicy + Lime Chicken

Servings: 6 / **Prep. Time:** 10min. / **Cook Time:** 3hr.

Ingredients:

- 1 ½ pound of chicken breast (boneless, skinless) about 4 halves
- 2 cups of chicken broth
- 3 tbsp. of lime juice
- 1 tbsp. of chili powder
- 1 tsp. of lime zest (grated)
- Fresh cilantro leaves

Instructions:

1. Put the chicken in 3-qt. Slow-Cooker. Merge the broth, chili powder, and lime juice, spill over the chicken. Cook overcovered, around 3hrs. on low before the chicken is soft.
2. Remove the chicken. Shred the meat using two forks until cold enough to handle; return to the Slow-Cooker. Stir in the zest of lime.
3. If needed, present with cilantro.

Calories: 132 / **Net Carb:** 1.5g / **Protein:** 23g / **Fats:** 3g / **Sugar:** 1g / **Fiber:** 1g

17. Slow-Cooker Coconut Quinoa Curry

Servings: 8 / **Prep. Time:** 20 min. / **Cook Time:** 4 hrs.

Ingredients:

- 1 medium (about 3 cups) peeled and chopped sweet potato
- 1 (2 cups) large broccoli crown
- ½ (1 cup) white onion diced
- 1 (15oz.) can of organic chickpeas, drained and rinsed
- 1 (28oz.) can of diced tomatoes
- 2 (14.5oz.) cans of coconut milk (either full fat or light)
- 1 ¼ cup of quinoa
- 2 (about 1 tbsp.) minced garlic cloves
- 1 tbsp. of freshly grated ginger
- 1 tbsp./1 tsp. of ground newly grated turmeric
- 2 tsp. of wheat-free tamari sauce
- 1 tsp. of miso or additional tamari
- 1 ½–1 tsp. of chili flakes

Instructions:

1. Add all the ingredients, beginning with one cup of water, to a crockpot. Stir until everything is incorporated fully.
2. Switch the Slow-Cooker on high and cook for 3–4 hours until the sweet potato cooks, and the curry thickens.

Calories: 289 / **Carbohydrates:** 20g / **Protein:** 6g / **Fat:** 22g / **Saturated Fat:** 19g / **Fiber:** 4g / **Sugar**: 4g

Chapter 3
Dinner Recipes

18. Slow-Cooker Sesame-Beef
Servings: 8 / **Prep. Time:** 5min. / Cook **Time:** 8hrs.
Ingredients:
- 3lb. (1.3kg) of roast-beef
- ½ cup (120ml) of coconut-aminos
- 1 cup (240ml) of water

For dipping-sauce:

- 2 tbsp. of sesame-oil (30ml)
- 1 tbsp. of sesame seeds (14g)
- 2 garlic cloves (peeled and minced)
- ¼ cup of coconut-aminos (60ml)

Instructions:
1. Put the beef, ½ cup of coconut aminos, and water into the Slow-Cooker and cook for 8 hours on low.
2. Remove the beef roast from the Slow-Cooker, let cool, and slice into thin slices.
3. Make the dipping sauce by mixing the sauce ingredients together.
4. Serve the beef slices with the dipping sauce.

Net Carbs: 4g / **Calories:** 374 / **Protein:** 46g / **Fat:** 16g / **Fiber:** 0g / Sugar: 0g/ **Cholesterol:** 132mg

19. Slow-Cooker Pizza Chicken
Servings: 5 / **Prep. Time:** 5min. / **Cook Time:** 8hrs.
Ingredients:
- 2 ½ pounds of chicken-breast (44oz.)
- Pizza-Sauce (20oz.), around 560g Low-Sodium/Low-Sugar
- 1 tsp. of garlic powder
- 1tsp. of oregano
- ½ green pepper (chopped)
- ½ sweet onion (chopped)
- ½ cup of mushrooms (chopped)
- (1 serving) pepperoni 28g slices (mini turkey)
- 1 cup of pizza cheese (112g reduced fat)

Instructions:

1. Cut beef, onions, mushrooms, and something else you desire.
2. Cover with a spray (non-stick) the Slow-Cooker.
3. Layer the pizza sauce with garlic powder, oregano, onions, mushrooms, and pepperoni slices.
4. Cover and simmer for 4–6hrs. on high; 6–8 hours at low.
5. Top with cheese.

Net Carbs: 10.8g / **Calories:** 398 / **Protein:** 68g / **Fiber:** 3g / **Fat:** 18g / **Sodium:** 88mg / **Sugar:** 7.6g

20. Crockpot Beef-Short-Ribs with Creamy Mushroom-Sauce (Low-carb, Keto)

Servings: 8 / **Prep. Time:** 5 min. / **Cook Time:** 8 hours

Ingredients:

- 2 pounds of beef-short-ribs
- 3oz. of cream cheese (softened)
- ½ cup of beef-broth
- 2 cups of white mushrooms
- 1 teaspoon of garlic powder
- 1 teaspoon of salt
- 1 teaspoon of black pepper

Instructions:

1. Beef-short-ribs are browned in a skillet.
2. In a crockpot, add cream cheese, garlic powder, beef broth, mushrooms, pepper, and salt.
3. In the Slow-Cooker, put beef-short-ribs on the mixture top.
4. Cover and simmer for 6–8hrs. on low, mixing gently every 1 to 2 hours.

Calories: 365 / **Protein:** 13g / **Fat:** 33g / **Saturated Fat:** 15g / **Sodium:** 422mg / **Net carb:** 1g / **Calcium:** 18g / **Cholesterol:** 74mg / **Iron:** 1.5mg

21. Slow-Cooker Italian-Beef

Servings: 6 / **Prep. Time:** 10 min. / **Cook Time:** 6 hrs. 15 min.

Ingredients:

- 4-pound of boneless-beef-chuck roast, fat-trimmed
- 2 tsp. of salt
- 1tsp. of pepper
- 2 tbsp. of olive oil
- 1 (12-ounces) jar of whole pepperoncini-peppers and their juice,
- 2 cups of beef stock
- 1 large onion, (peeled sliced, cut in half)
- 5 large garlic cloves, (peeled n chopped)
- 2 tbsp. of dried Italian-seasonings
- 1 tsp. of onion-powder
- 1 bay-leaf

Instructions:

1. Add the beef stock, onion, garlic, pepperoncini-peppers, onion powder, Italian seasonings, and bay leaf. Blend to mix these components.
2. Cut the beef into 6-inch chunks of even size, also cut the fat. Add 2tsp. of salt and 1 tsp. of pepper to the pieces.
3. To a big skillet, add olive oil and turn high the heat. When the pan is hot, add the meat carefully and sear on every side, spinning every 2–3min. Remove meat from the pan and put it in the crockpot along with any meat searing pan juices. Try getting all the meat in the liquid in a single layer and cover it with the lid.
4. Turn down the crockpot to low, and cook for 6 hrs.
5. Open the cover and turn warm the crockpot. Drain the cooking liquid in a bowl (around 3–4 cups should be it). Eliminate any oily fat. Then pour in the cooking liquid to remove any pieces and bits through a strainer. The juice is then added to the sauté pan at simmer heat and then cook for 4 to 5 mins. Move the decreased liquid for cooking to a gravy or serving bowl.
6. Take the Italian beef off from the crockpot, use two forks to remove or shred it. Put it on a large platter, then add the pepperoncini and onions for topping. Remove any of the pepperoncini stems, and finish with shredded provolone, Italian blend, or mozzarella cheese. In the microwave, heat the plate to melt the cheese if needed.

7. Serve as a dipping sauce with the cooking juice and combine with your favorite veggies such as cauliflower-rice, zucchini-noodles, or spaghetti-squash. Or you can use your favorite sandwich rolls to make sub-sandwiches, hoagies, sliders, etc. if you are not on a low-carb diet.

Calories: 314 / **Protein:** 31g / **Sodium:** 98mg / **Fat:** 26g / **Net carb:** 5g / **Sugar:** 3g / **Fiber:** 1g

22. (Keto) Slow-Cooker Tri-Tip

Servings: 4 / **Prep. Time:** 5 min. / **Cook Time:** 5 hours

Ingredients:

- 1 tri-tip roast (2 and a half lb. or 1.2kg)
- 2 tbsp. of homemade Montreal-steak seasoning
- 3 ounces of salted butter

Instructions

1. Place two sheets of overlapping aluminum foil and put the tri-tip.
2. Sprinkle all over the seasoning, then add the butter on top.
3. Cover in the foil and put it in the Slow-Cooker.
4. Cook on high for 5 hours or at low for 8–9 hours.
5. Detach gently from Slow-Cooker and shred or slice.
6. Serve, drizzled with a few cooking juices.

Net Carbs: 0.5g / **Calories:** 516 / **Protein:** 48g / **Cholesterol:** 193mg / **Saturated Fat:** 17g

23. Slow-Cooker (Keto) Meatball-Casserole

Servings: 8 / **Prep. Time:** 5 min. / **Cook Time:** 2 hours 15 minutes

Ingredients:

- 1 head of cabbage (chopped)
- 1 pound of ground beef
- 1 pound of spicy-pork sausage
- 1 cup of mozzarella-shredded
- 1/3 cup of grated parmesan
- ½ cup of pork-rinds (crushed)
- 2 eggs
- 2 tsp. of onion-powder
- 2 tsp. of garlic-minced
- ½ tsp. of Italian-seasoning
- 1 jar of low-carb marinara-sauce
- 2 cups of mozzarella
- Basil-garnish

Instructions:

1. In a big bowl, combine the ground beef, parmesan, ham, mozzarella, pork rinds, onion powder, garlic, Italian seasoning, and eggs.
2. Place cabbage at the bottom of the crockpot casserole.
3. Pour the red sauce uniformly over the top.
4. Add meatballs to the top.
5. Cook 3–4 hours.
6. Sprinkle the mozzarella on cooked meatballs and give 10–15min. to melt.
7. Add basil to garnish.

Net Carbs: 3.8g / **Calories:** 521 / **Protein:** 45.7g / **Fat:** 35.1g / **Fiber:** 0.1g / **Sugar:** 1.3g

24. (Low-carb) Slow-Cooker Butter-Chicken

Servings: 4 / **Prep. Time:** 15min. / **Cook Time:** 7 hrs.

Ingredients:

- 2 tablespoons (26g or 0.9oz.) of ghee
- 1 medium (110g or 3.88oz.) onion
- 3 (9g or 0.32oz.) garlic cloves
- 3 tbsp. (18g or 0.63oz.) of ginger
- 1 tbsp. garam-masala (Punjabi)
- 6 tbsp. (98g or 3.47oz.) of tomato-paste
- 1 ½ tsp. (9g or 0.32oz.) of kosher salt
- 3 pounds (1361g or 48 oz.) of chicken breasts
- 1 tbsp. (15g or 0.54 oz.) of lime juice (raw)
- 1 cup of coconut milk
- ½ cup (120g or 4.23oz.) of chicken-stock
- ⅛ cup (2g or 0.07oz.) of cilantro, raw, coriander-leaves

Instructions:

1. Heat a med-sauté pan over med-high heat. Once the pan is heated, add ghee. Then add the minced garlic, diced onion, garam masala, and minced ginger to the mixture. Stir until the spices are fragrant, and the onions start browning. Add the tomato paste and simmer until dark. Add salt.
2. Dice the chicken into 2-inches pieces and add the lime zest, lime juice, chicken stock, and coconut milk to the bottom of a Slow-Cooker (4-quart). Add the mixture of onion and tomato paste to the Slow-Cooker too. Mix together. Then set to low, Slow-Cooker and cook until chicken is tender for 7–8 hours.
3. With cauliflower rice, serve and finish with cilantro.

Net Carbs: 9.2g / **Calories:** 767 / **Protein:** 107g / **Fat:** 29g / **Fiber:** 1.6g / **Sugar:** 6.3g

25. Low-Carb Mushroom Lover's Pot Roast Slow-Cooker

Servings: 8 / **Prep. Time:** 15 min. / **Cook Time:** 4 hrs.

Ingredients:

- 2 mushroom stock in cubes
- 2 tablespoon of mushroom stock base
- ½ cup of water
- 3 ½ pound of chuck roast, fat trimmed
- 2 tablespoon of steak rub
- 1 teaspoon of onion powder
- ¾ teaspoon of kosher salt
- ½ teaspoon of ground pepper fresh
- 1 tablespoon of olive oil
- 1 to ½ pounds of cremini mushrooms

Instructions

1. Put the stock base or mushroom cubes in a measuring cup with water (1/2 cup) and microwave until the bottom of the mushroom has dissolved in the water, around one min. Stir to blend.
2. Trim the roast, removing most of the fat, even though the roast needs to be split into pieces to take off the fat. (You can trim less aggressively if you want the flavor of the beef fat.)
3. The rub steak is mixed with onion powder, black pepper, and salt. With the spice mix, rub every side of the beef generously.
4. Heat the oil in a frying pan, non-stick or cast-iron, and brown the meat on both sides. It will take around 5–7mins. to do this, don't hurry through the browning stage. Put it in the Slow-Cooker, when meat is well browned.
5. For 1–2 minutes, pour the mixture of mushroom stock in the frying pan and on the high cook, scraping with turner to extract any brown bits from the pan bottom. In the Slow-Cooker over the meat, pour the liquid.
6. Cook for 3 hours on high.
7. Clean and chop the mushrooms in thick slices. Place mushrooms in the crockpot over the meat and cook for another 45–60 minutes, or until the meat is tender and the mushrooms are cooked as you pierce it with some fork.
8. With a slotted spoon, scoop the meat and mushrooms out; place in a bowl the mushrooms and on a cutting board, the meat.
9. To minimize and enhance the flavor, strain the juice, then taste to see whether it require simmer.
10. Cut the meat and serve it with mushrooms. **Calories:** 664 / **Total Fat:** 40g / **Saturated Fat:** 16g / **Carbs:** 6g / **Fiber:** 1g / **Sugar:** 3g / Protein: 69g

26. Green Chile Beef Shredded Cabbage Bowl with Avocado Salsa

Servings: 6 / **Prep. Time:** 20 min. / **Cook Time:** 4 hrs.

Ingredients:

- 3 lb. of beef chuck roast
- 1 tbsp. of Kalyn's taco seasoning
- 2 tsp. of olive oil (depending on your pan)
- 2 cans of green chiles diced with juice

Avocado salsa ingredients:

- 2 large avocados, diced
- 1 medium diced poblano (pasilla) pepper
- 1 tbsp. of lime juice fresh-squeezed
- 1 tbsp. of olive oil extra-virgin
- 1/2 cup of finely chopped cilantro

Instructions:

1. Trim any noticeable fat from the chuck roast and other unwanted parts and cut in thick strips.
2. Apply beef strips with taco seasoning. Heat the oil in a big, heavy frying pan and brown both sides of the beef well.
3. In the Slow-Cooker, put the strips of browned beef and pour the green chiles (diced) and the juice of the can.
4. Cook for 3–4 hours on high, or until the beef easily shreds apart.
5. Use a wide slotted spoon to move it to a cutting board when the beef is cooked, then keep the liquid in the crockpot. Shred beef apart with two forks and placed it back in the Slow-Cooker for it to absorb the juices, and to hold it warm when Preparing slaw to salsa for the cabbages.
6. In very thin strips, cut the cabbage. Slice the green onions.
7. To Prepare the dressing, whisk the mayo, green tabasco sauce, and lime juice together. Then add the green onions and cabbage in a bowl and mix with the dressing.
8. Peel the avocado and cut it, put it in a bowl, and toss with lime juice. Chop the cilantro/green onion) and the Poblano chili finely and then add to the avocado. Drizzle over the olive oil and toss again softly.
9. Put a layer of slaw to assemble the bowl, then a generous quantity of the beef (spicy), topped with a few spoonfuls of avocado salsa.

Fat: 37g / **Carbohydrates:** 16.6g / **Sugar:** 9g / **Fiber:** 7g / **Protein:** 59g

Chapter 4
Dessert Recipes

27. Slow-Cooker Low-carb Pumpkin Cake

Servings: 10 / **Prep. Time:** 5 min. / **Cook Time:** 1 hr. 30 min.

Ingredients:

- 4 tablespoons of melted butter
- 4 beaten eggs
- ¾ cup of blanched almond flour
- 2 teaspoons of baking powder
- 1 teaspoon of cinnamon powder
- 1 teaspoon of pumpkin pie spice
- ½ cup of pure pumpkin
- ½ cup of brown sugar

Instructions:

1. Grease the Slow-Cooker with the cooking spray.
2. Beat the eggs in a wide bowl, then add the remainder of the ingredients, then mixed well.
3. In the Slow-Cooker, pour it and bake for around 1 1/2 hours on high.
4. Depending on the Slow-Cooker, cooking times can differ. After 1 1/2 hour, check it out and insert a toothpick in the cake middle. If not cooked, then cook for 10 more minutes and again insert the toothpick to check it.
5. Top with candied pecans, cream cheese, or whipped cream. For a nice, low-carb breakfast, eat it.

Calories: 112 / **Fat:** 9.5g / **Carbs:** 3.5g / **Fiber:** 1.4g / **Protein:** 3.9g / **Net Carbs:** 2.1g

28. Slow-Cooker Low-carb Mint Chocolate Cake

Servings: 8 / **Prep. Time:** 10 min. / **Cook Time:** 3 hrs.

Ingredients:

- 1 cup (+ 2 tbs.) of almond flour
- ½ cup of sweetener, e.g., Lakanto
- ⅓ cup of unsweetened cocoa powder
- 1 ½ tsp. of baking powder
- ¼ tsp. of salt
- 3 beaten eggs
- 6 tbs. of unsalted butter, melted and cooled
- ⅔ cup of unsweetened almond milk
- ½ tsp. of peppermint extract
- ⅓ cup of mini chocolate chips low-carb, e.g., Lily's

Instructions:

1. In a bowl, mix the almond flour, unsweetened cocoa powder, sweetener, salt, and baking powder.
2. Add melted butter, beaten eggs, unsweetened almond milk, peppermint extract, and chocolate chips (low-carb).
3. Pour the batter into a Slow-Cooker greased bowl and set it to simmer for 2–3 hours at low heat.
4. Leave the cake for 30 minutes to cool, then serve.

Net Carbs: 4g Per Serving / **Calories:** 214 / **Fat:** 19g / **Carbs**: 8g / **Fiber:** 4g / **Protein:** 6g

29. Slow-Cooker Dark Chocolate Cake

Servings: 10 / **Prep. Time:** 10 min. / **Cook Time:** 3 hrs.

Ingredients:

- 1 cup + 2 tbsp. of almond flour
- ½ cup of swerve granular
- ½ cup of cocoa powder
- 3 tbsp. of whey protein powder unflavored
- 1 ½ tsp. of baking powder
- ¼ tsp. of salt
- 6 tbsp. of butter melted
- 3 large eggs
- 2/3 cup of unsweetened almond milk
- ¾ tsp. of vanilla extract
- 1/3 cup of chocolate chips sugar-free (optional)

Instructions:

1. Grease a 6 quarters Slow-Cooker insert correctly.
2. Whisk together, sweetener, almond flour, cocoa powder, salt, whey protein, and baking powder in a med bowl.
3. Stir in the butter, eggs, vanilla extract, and almond milk until well mixed then, add the chocolate chips.
4. Pour in a made insert and cook for 2–2 1/2 hours on low. At 2 hours, it'll be gooey and a pudding cake-like, and at 2 1/2 hours, cakier.
5. Switch off the Slow-Cooker and let it cool for 20 to 30 mins., then slice and serve. Serve with whipped cream.

Calories: 205 / **Fat:** 17g / **Carbohydrates:** 8.4g / **Fiber:** 4.1g / **Protein:** 7.4g

30. Slow-Cooker Low-Carb Chocolate Lava Cake

Servings: 5 / **Prep. Time:** 15 min. / **Cook Time:** 2 hrs. 30 min.

Ingredients:

Chocolate Lava Cake:

- 100g of almond meal/flour
- 50g of coconut flour
- 25g of cocoa powder
- 4 tbsp. of granulated sweetener of choice
- 2 tsp. of baking powder
- ¼ tsp. of salt
- 60g of dark chocolate chips sugar-free
- 3 eggs
- 1 egg white
- 180ml of almond milk unsweetened
- 1 tsp. of vanilla
- 4 tbsp. of unsalted melted butter

Chocolate Sauce:

- 125ml of warm water
- 2 tbsp of cocoa powder
- 1 tbsp. of granulated sweetener of choice

Instructions:

1. On the Slow-Cooker, grease the liner.
2. Mix wet ingredients for the cake in a bowl. Through a fine-mesh sieve or sifter, sift the dry ingredients into the wet ingredients. Mix in the wet and dry ingredients.
3. In the Slow-Cooker, add the batter into it and spread it. Sprinkle with the chocolate chips over the batter. Mix the chocolate sauce in a different cup, then pour over the batter, don't mix it in. Let the chocolate sauce stay on top of the batter.
4. Get the Slow-Cooker covered. Cook the cake at a low setting for 2 to 2 ½ hrs. Depending on the Slow-Cooker size, the processing period varies, so keep a close eye. It's finished with a glossy top and seems fudgy. It shouldn't make the cake look dry. Scoop out the cake and serve in a bowl layered with whipped cream and berries.

Calories: 359 / **Carbohydrates:** 17g / **Protein:** 11g / **Fat:** 28g / **Fiber:** 9g / **Sugar:** 2g / **Net Carbs:** 8g

31. Crockpot Sugar-Free Dairy-Free Fudge

Servings: 30 / **Prep. Time:** 5 min. / **Cook Time:** 2 hrs.

Ingredients:

- 2 ½ cups of chocolate chips sugar-free
- 1/3 cup of coconut milk
- 1 tsp. of pure vanilla extract
- Salt
- 2 teaspoons of liquid vanilla stevia (optional)

Instructions:

1. In a tiny 3 or 4 quarter crockpot, mix in coconut milk, vanilla, chocolate chips, stevia, and salt.
2. Cover and simmer for 2 hours on low.
3. Turn off, uncover, and let stay for 30 mins. to 1 hour.
4. For 5 minutes, stir well until smooth.
5. Line a one-quarter parchment paper casserole dish and place the mixture in.
6. Refrigerate for 30 minutes or until solid.

Calories: 65 / **Fat:** 5g / **Saturated Fat:** 3g / **Carbohydrates:** 2g / **Protein:** 1g

32. Slow-Cooker Keto Maple Custard

Servings: 6 / **Prep. Time:** 10 min. / **Cook Time:** 4 hrs.

Ingredients:

- 2 egg yolks
- 2 eggs
- 1 cup of heavy cream
- ½ cup of full fat canned coconut milk
- ¼ cup of swerve brown sugar
- 1 tsp. of maple extract
- ¼ tsp. of salt
- ½ tsp. of cinnamon

Instructions:

1. Combine all ingredients, then on med-high blend it on the mixer until well mixed.
2. Grease six ramekins with the capacity of 4 ounces and pour the batter equally into each one, filling just 3/4 way full, effectively around 3 ounces filled.

3. On the Slow-Cooker bottom, place four ramekins. Carefully place the other two on one side of the Slow-Cooker and partially on the ends of the ramekins.
4. Cover the lid and cook on high for 2 hours or until the middle is fine, but always jiggly in the core.
5. Remove now and cool for 1 hour at room temperature, then put in the refrigerator for 2 hours to chill.
6. Enjoy with some whipped cream sugar-free and cinnamon sprinkle.

Net carbs: 1g / **Calories:** 212 / **Fat:** 21g / **Saturated Fat:** 13g / **Carbohydrates:** 2g / **Fiber:** 1g / **Sugar:** 1g / **Protein:** 4g

33. Easy Slow-Cooker Lemon Custard

Servings: 4 / **Prep. Time:** 10 min. / **Cook Time:** 3 hrs.

Ingredients:

- 5 large egg yolks
- ¼ cup of lemon juice freshly squeezed
- 1 tbsp. of lemon zest
- 1 tsp. of vanilla extract
- ½ tsp. of liquid stevia
- 2 cups of whipping cream/coconut cream
- Whipped cream lightly sweetened/whipped coconut cream

Instructions:

1. Whisk the egg yolks, lemon zest, lemon juice, vanilla, and liquid stevia together in a bowl.
2. Whisk the heavy cream and split the mixture into four little jars or ramekins.
3. Place a rack in the Slow-Cooker bottom and place ramekins. Add sufficient water to touch the ramekins halfway up the sides.
4. Cover and cook for 3 hrs. on low.
5. Remove now the ramekins and allow them cool at room temperature, cool now in the refrigerator fully (about 3 hrs.). Top and serve with whipped cream.

Calories: 319 / **Fat:** 30g / **Carbohydrates:** 3g / **Protein:** 7g

34. Crockpot Sugar-Free Pumpkin Pie Bars

Servings: 16 bars / **Prep. Time:** 15 min. / **Cook Time:** 3 hrs.

Ingredients:

Crust:

- ¾ cup of unsweetened shredded coconut
- ¼ cup of unsweetened cocoa powder
- ½ cup of raw sunflower seeds/sunflower seed flour
- ¼ teaspoon of salt
- ¼ cup of swerve confectioners
- 4 tablespoons of unsalted butter softened

Filling:

- 1 can of pumpkin puree
- 1 cup of heavy cream
- 6 eggs
- 1/2 teaspoon of salt
- 1 tablespoon of vanilla extract
- 1 tablespoon of pumpkin pie spice
- 2 teaspoons of cinnamon liquid stevia

Instructions:

Crust:

1. Put all the crust ingredients in the food processor and process until fine crumbs.
2. Grease a Slow-Cooker's bottom.
3. Place the crust mixture as uniformly as possible in the Slow-Cooker bottom.

Filling:

1. Add the filling ingredients to the stand mixer, then blend until well mixed.
2. If needed, stir in or top with additional chocolate chips.
3. Pour the mix on the crust.
4. Cover and boil for 3 hours at low.
5. Uncover and cool for 30 min., then refrigerate the whole Slow-Cooker for 3 hours at least.
6. Cut on and serve with whipped cream free of sugar.

Net Carbs: 4g / **Calories:** 169 / **Fat:** 15g / **Saturated Fat:** 8g / **Carbohydrates:** 6g / **Fiber:** 2g / **Sugar:** 2g / **Protein:** 4g

35. Crockpot Blueberry Lemon Custard Cake

Servings: 12 / **Prep. Time:** 15 min. / **Cook Time:** 3 hrs.

Ingredients:

- 6 Eggs separated
- ½ cup of Coconut flour
- 2 tsp. of Lemon zest
- 1/3 cup of Lemon juice
- 1 tsp. of Lemon liquid stevia
- ½ cup of Swerve confectioner's sweetener
- ½ tsp. of Salt
- 2 cups of Heavy cream
- 1/2 cup of Fresh blueberries

Instructions:

1. Place the egg whites in a stand mixer and whip until the peaks are stiff.
2. Whisk together the yolks and the remaining ingredients in another dish, except for the blueberries.
3. Fold the whites of the egg into the mixture a few at a time before you have all combined.
4. Grease the Slow-Cooker and dump it in the pot with the mixture.
5. Sprinkle over the blueberries on the batter.
6. Cover and cook for 3 hours or until a clean toothpick comes out.
7. Enable to cool for 1 hour with the cover off, then put in the refrigerator to cool for 2 hrs. or overnight.
8. Serve cold, with whipped cream sugar-free if needed.

   Net Carbs: 3g / **Calories:** 191 / **Fat:** 17g / **Saturated Fat:** 10g / **Carbohydrates:** 4g / **Fiber:** 1g / **Protein:** 4g

36. Slow-Cooker Raspberry Cream Cheese Coffee Cake

Servings: 12 / **Prep. Time:** 15 min. / **Cook Time:** 4 hrs.

Ingredients:

Cake batter:
- 1 ¼ cup of almond flour
- ½ cup of swerve sweetener
- ¼ cup of coconut flour
- ¼ cup of organic valley vanilla protein powder
- 1 ½ tsp. of baking powder
- ¼ tsp. of salt
- 3 large eggs
- 6 tbsp. of butter melted organic valley pasture
- 2/3 cup of water
- 1/2 tsp. of vanilla extract

Filling:
- 8 ounces of organic valley cream cheese
- 1/3 cup of powdered swerve sweetener
- 1 large egg
- 2 tbsp. of organic valley whipping cream
- 1 ½ cup of fresh raspberries

Instructions:

1. Grease the insert well of a crockpot (6 quarts).
2. Combine the sweetener, almond flour, coconut flour, salt protein powder, and baking powder in a med-bowl for the cake batter. Add the eggs, the melted butter, and water until well mixed. When creating the filling, set aside.
3. Beat with the sweetener the cream cheese until smooth for filling. Beat until well mixed the egg, vanilla extract, and whipping cream.
4. Spread the batter nearly two thirds into a ready Slow-Cooker to form the cake, smoothing the surface with an offset spatula or knife.
5. Put the mixture of cream cheese into the pan over the batter and distribute uniformly. Sprinkle the raspberries. Dot the leftover batter in tiny spoonful over the filling, allowing some filling to show.
6. Bake for 3 to 4 hrs. on low or until the sides are golden brown and the filling is only barely set in the center (when shaken, it can jiggle a bit). Switch the Slow-Cooker off, and the ceramic insert is removed. Before serving, allow it to cool.

Calories: 239 / **Fat:** 19.18g / **Carbohydrates:** 6.95g / **Fiber:** 3.08g / **Protein:** 7.54g

Chapter Five
Vegetable recipes

37. Slow-Cooker Eggplant Parmesan (Breakfast)

Servings: 12 / **Prep. Time:** 25 min. / **Cook Time:** 8 hrs.

Ingredients:

- 4 pounds of eggplant
- 1 tablespoon of salt
- 3 large eggs
- ¼ cup of milk of choice
- 1 ½ cup of gluten-free breadcrumbs
- 3 ounces of vegetarian parmesan cheese/vegan parmesan
- 2 teaspoons of Italian seasoning
- 4 cups of marinara sauce
- 16 ounces of mozzarella cheese sliced/shredded Daiya
- fresh basil for topping

Instructions:

1. Peel and cut the eggplant into 1/3" rounds. Layer in the colander, sprinkling salt on each layer. Enable 30 minutes to rest, and pat dry then.
2. Cover the Slow-Cooker bottom with ½ cup sauce. In a bowl, whisk the milk and eggs together. Now in a different bowl, stir together the parmesan cheese, breadcrumbs, and Italian seasoning. In the egg mixture, dip the eggplant and in the breadcrumbs.
3. 1/3 of the slices layer in the crockpot. Cover with 1 cup of sauce and cheese (mozzarella). Repeat two more layers. Cook for 8 hours, on low.
4. Top with basil leaves if needed.

Calories: 258 / **Carbohydrates:** 23g / **Protein:** 16g / **Fat:** 12g / **Saturated Fat:** 6g / **Fiber:** 6g / **Sugar:** 9g

38. Slow-Cooker Mac and Cheese (breakfast)

Servings: 8 / **Prep. Time:** 15 min. / **Cook Time:** 2 hrs.

Ingredients:

- 1 lb. of cavatappi pasta/corkscrew-shaped pasta
- 1/4 cup of butter cut into cubes
- 1 (12 ounces) can of evaporated milk
- 1 ½ cups of half and half
- 4 cups of shredded cheddar cheese
- ½ lb. of orange American cheese block cut in cubes (8 ounces)
- ½ teaspoon of salt
- ¼ teaspoon of pepper
- ¼ teaspoon of onion powder
- ¼ teaspoon of paprika
- Cooking spray
- 2 teaspoons of chopped parsley to garnish (optional)

Instructions

1. Cook the pasta for 2 extra minutes than the label instructions in boiling water.
2. Use a cooking spray to coat a 4 to 6-quart crockpot. In the crockpot, put the noodles, and add butter. Remove until the butter has covered the noodles.
3. Add American cheese, cheddar cheese, pepper, salt, onion powder, and paprika, half and half, and evaporated milk.
4. Until combined, stir.
5. Cover and cook for 1 ½–2 hrs. on low. Remove after 30 min.
6. At the end of cooking time, whisk until the noodles are coated with a smooth sauce. If needed, topped with parsley.

Calories: 571 / **Carbohydrates:** 51g / **Protein:** 25g / **Fat:** 28g / **Saturated Fat:** 17g / **Fiber:** 1g / **Sugar:** 10g

39. Eggs Over Cauliflower Hash (Breakfast)

Servings: 4 / **Prep. Time:** 15min. / **Cook Time:** 1hr. 45min.

Ingredients:

- 16 ounces (approximately 4 cups) of one package of riced-cauliflower
- 2 eggs
- 3 tbsp. of egg-white 1 or liquid-egg whites
- ¼ teaspoon garlic powder
- ½ tsp. of kosher salt
- ½ tsp. of black pepper
- ½ cup of cheddar-cheese (reduced fat 2%)
- 1 (about 1/4 cup) large scallion (chopped)
- ¼ cup of white-wholewheat flour (or gluten-free flour)
- 4 eggs
- Salt and pepper

Instructions:

1. Add cauliflower rice, microwave for 3min. in a large bowl.
2. To suck out the extra water, use paper towels or cheesecloth.
3. Mix the cauliflower in a wide bowl with all the ingredients (except for the last 4 eggs) and blend well.
4. Spray a non-stick cooking spray well on a Slow-Cooker. Add a mixture of cauliflower and scatter, flattening the center and enabling some to go to the sides somewhat.
5. Cook them on high for 1hr 15 min.
6. Put 4 eggs on top of the cauliflower and continue to cook for further 20–30 mins. depending on whether you like the yolks to be runny or firm. Add salt and pepper.
7. Offer with Harissa, Tzatziki, or some other seasoning.

Net Carbs: 13g / **Calories:** 220 / **Protein:** 18g / **Fats:** 10g / **Cholesterol:** 290mg / **Fiber:** 4g / **Sodium:** 490mg

40. Slow-Cooker Butternut Squash Dal (Lunch)

Servings: 6 / **Prep. Time:** 10 min. / **Cook Time:** 3 hrs.

Ingredients:

- 1 tbsp. of olive oil
- 2 diced small yellow onions
- 4 minced cloves garlic
- 1 small butternut squash
- 1 ½ cups of dry red lentils
- 1 (400ml) can of coconut milk
- 1 (796ml) can of diced tomatoes
- 1 tbsp. of turmeric
- 1 tbsp. of curry powder
- 1 tsp. of chili powder
- 1 tsp. of salt
- ¼ tsp. of pepper
- 2 cups of spinach chopped
- For garnish cilantro and sesame seeds

Basmati rice:

- 1 cup of basmati rice
- 1 ¼ cup of water
- 1 tsp. of butter
- 1 of pinch salt

Instructions:

1. Add to Slow-Cooker all ingredients, except for garnishes, spinach, and rice.
2. Cook 4 hours on high, or 8 hours on average. Meanwhile, on the stovetop or in a rice cooker, cook basmati rice as per label instructions.
3. Stir in spinach, then plate with rice, garnish with cilantro and sesame seeds, once dal is done. Enjoy it now.

Calories: 383 / **Carbohydrates:** 72g / **Protein:** 16g / **Fat:** 4g / **Saturated Fat:** 1g / **Fiber:** 18g / **Sugar:** 5g

41. Slow-Cooker Cheesy Butternut Squash Macaroni (Lunch)

Servings: 2 / **Prep. Time:** 15 min. / **Cook Time:** 8 hrs.

Ingredients:

For the morning:

- 1 ½ cups (210g) of cubed butternut squash other winter squash
- ½ cup (90g) of chopped tomatoes
- 1 ½ cups (355ml) of water
- 2 minced cloves of garlic
- 3 (3-inch 7.5cm) sprigs fresh thyme
- 1 ½ tsp. (1.5g) of dried thyme
- 1 (2-inch 5cm) sprig of fresh rosemary
- ½ teaspoon of dried rosemary

For the evening:

- ¼ cup (24g) of nutritional yeast flakes
- ½ cup (120–235ml) of unsweetened non-dairy milk
- 1 ½ cups (158g) of uncooked whole-wheat macaroni
- Salt and pepper to taste

Instructions:

1. **In the morning:** Add ingredients to the crockpot in the morning. On low, cook for 7–9 hours.
2. 30 to 45 min. until serving, purée the nutritional yeast, ½ cup non-dairy milk (120ml,) and the Slow-Cooker content in a blender. In the Slow-Cooker, put the mixture back and switch it to high. Add the macaroni, then cover, and simmer for 20 min.
3. If the sauce is too heavy, mix well, and add more cream. Cook for another 15 to 25 minutes, or until the pasta is al dente. Garnish with salt and pepper.
4. Make sure you check the pasta every 10 minutes or so before you get nice in your Slow-Cooker to gauge how fast it can cook. In the small size Slow-Cooker, it heats quicker.

Calories: 447 / **Carbohydrates:** 96g / **Protein:** 19g / **Fat:** 1g / **Fiber:** 4g / **Sugar:** 3g

42. Super Easy Skinny Veggie Crockpot Lasagna (Lunch)

Servings: 9 / **Prep. Time:** 30 min. / **Cook Time:** 6 hrs.

Ingredients:

- 2 (24-ounce) cans of Italian tomato sauce jars
- 9 thick lasagna noodles with wavy edges
- 24 ounces of ricotta cheese/cottage cheese part-skim
- 3–4 cups of chopped vegetables
- Pesto
- 2 cups of shredded mozzarella/provolone cheese
- For topping Parmesan cheese
- For topping Fresh parsley

Instructions:

1. Spray non-stick cooking spray onto the crockpot. Spread tomato sauce (1/2 cup) to the bottom such that noodles do not stick together.
2. Break the noodles in such a way that they cover the base and fit also. They're just going to appear weird—not a huge deal. Cover with around a third of the veggies, ricotta, pesto, cheese, sauce, and finish with the noodles. For a total of three top layers, repeat the layers 2 more times. Cover that with a noodles layer, a thin sauce layer, and a little shredded cheese on top.
3. Cover and cook for 3 hrs. on high or 5–6 hrs. on low. Switch off the crockpot entirely, then let the lasagna rest for an hour, at least. This enables all the moisture to get absorbed in the lasagna, and if it is not done, then it's actually going to be something lasagna soup like—still healthy, just not great. You can either scoop out bits or just break them with a knife like a regular lasagna.

Total Fat: 12.6g / **Cholesterol:** 38.8mg / **Total Carbohydrate:** 39.4g / **Dietary Fiber:** 3.9g / **Sugars:** 8.8g / **Protein:** 19.4g

43. Vegetarian Lentil Tortilla Soup (Dinner)

Servings: 6 / **Prep. Time:** 10 min. / **Cook Time:** 7–8 hrs.

Ingredients:

- 1 cup of diced onion
- 1 tsp. of avocado oil
- 1 bell pepper diced
- 1 jalapeno pepper diced
- 2.5 cups of vegetable broth (or chicken broth)
- 15 oz. of tomato sauce canned or crushed tomatoes
- ½ cup of mild/medium salsa verde
- 1 tbsp. of tomato paste
- 15 oz. can of black beans (drained + rinsed)
- 15 oz. can of pinto beans (drained + rinsed)
- 1 cup of corn (canned, fresh, or frozen)
- ¾ cup of dried red lentils
- ½ tsp. of chili powder
- ½ tsp. of garlic powder
- ½ tsp. of cumin
- ¼ tsp. of cayenne pepper
- ¼–½ cup of heavy cream (optional)
- Salt and pepper

Instructions:

1. Chop the vegetables first, then weigh the ingredients. That will make it all super easy to toss together.
2. Next, incorporate all but the heavy cream and toppings.
3. Cook for 4–6 hours on high, or 7–8 hours on medium, until dried lentils are cooked through, and vegetables are soft. After 5 hours on the maximum.
4. Swirl in the milk, add the toppings you want, and plunge.

Calories: 284 / **Fat:** 2g / **Carbohydrates:** 52g / **Fiber:** 17g / **Sugar:** 9g / **Protein**: 15g

44. Slow-Cooker Enchilada Quinoa Bake (Dinner)

Servings: 6 / **Prep. Time:** 10 min. / **Cook Time:** 3 hrs.

Ingredients:

- 1 tbsp. of canola oil
- 1 ¼ cups (1 medium) of chopped yellow onion
- 1 ¼ cups of (1 medium) red bell pepper chopped
- 3 minced cloves of garlic
- 1 ½ cups of dry quinoa
- 2 ¼ cups of vegetable broth
- 1 (14.5 oz.) can of undrained tomatoes with green chilies
- 1 (8 oz.) can of tomato sauce
- 2 tbsp. of chili powder
- 1 ½ tsp. of ground cumin
- Salt and black pepper freshly ground
- 1 (14.5 oz.) can of drained and rinsed black beans
- 1 (14.5 oz.) can of drained and rinsed pinto beans
- 1 ½ cups of frozen corn
- 1 ½ cups of cheddar/Monterey jack/Mexican blend cheese

Instructions:

1. Heat the canola oil over medium to high heat in a skillet. Add the bell pepper and onion and sauté for 3 mins. Add garlic and begin to sauté for 30 seconds. Pour the mixture now.
2. Stir the quinoa, canned tomatoes, vegetable broth, tomato sauce, chili powder, cumin, and season with salt and pepper.
3. Cover and cook at high heat around 2 hours 45 min.–3 hours 15 mins. It depends on the cooker.
4. Add the mixture of corn, pinto beans, and black beans and toss. Sprinkle with cheese at the top. Cover and cook until heated, around 10 to 15 mins. longer, when the cheese has melted. With preferred toppings, serve warm.

Calories: 519 / **Fat:** 16g / **Saturated Fat:** 6g / **Carbohydrates:** 74g / **Fiber:** 16g / **Sugar:** 9g / **Protein:** 24g

45. Slow-Cooker Vegetarian Chili Mac (Dinner)

Servings: 6 / **Prep. Time:** 15 min. / **Cook Time:** 4 hrs.

Ingredients:

- 1 medium chopped onion
- 1 chopped red bell pepper
- 15 ounces can of rinsed and drained pinto beans
- 15 ounces can of rinsed and drained kidney beans
- 28 ounces can of crushed tomatoes
- 1 ½ tablespoon of chili powder
- 2 teaspoons of cumin
- ½ teaspoon of salt
- 1/8 teaspoon of black pepper
- 2 cups of vegetable broth
- 8 ounces of elbow macaroni pasta whole wheat uncooked
- 1 ½ cups about 6 oz of cheddar cheese, divided
- For serving chopped green onions

Instructions:

1. Put all ingredients in a Slow-Cooker, except green onions, pasta, and cheese. Stir to mix. Cover and simmer for 4 hours on high heat or 6–8 hours on low heat.
2. Stir in the pasta and start to cook for 15–20 mins., before the pasta is thoroughly cooked. Stir in one cup of cheese.
3. Serve with leftover cheese and green onions.

Calories: 428 / **Carbohydrates:** 64g / **Protein:** 22g / **Fat:** 16g / **Saturated Fat:** 6g / **Fiber:** 11g / **Sugar:** 10g

46. Quinoa Black Bean Crockpot Stuffed Peppers (Dinner)

Servings: 6 / **Prep. Time:** 10 min. / **Cook Time:** 4 hrs.

Ingredients:

- 6 bell peppers
- 1 cup of uncooked quinoa, rinsed
- 1 (14 ounces) can of rinsed and drained black beans
- 1 (14 ounces) can of refried beans
- 1 1/2 cups of red enchilada sauce
- 1 teaspoon of cumin
- 1 teaspoon of chili powder
- 1 teaspoon of onion powder
- ½ teaspoon of garlic salt
- 1 ½ cups of shredded pepper jack cheese

Instructions:

1. Cut the tops of the peppers off and pull the seeds and ribs out.
2. Combine the beans, quinoa, spices, enchilada sauce, and one cup of cheese in a complete dish. Fill up the quinoa mixture with each pepper.
3. In a crockpot bottom, add ½ cup of water. In the crockpot, put the peppers, so they are in the water. Cover and cook for 6 hours on low, or 3 hours on high. Remove the cover, spread the leftover cheese over the pepper tops, and cover the cheese again to melt.
4. Serve with something you desire. These are fantastic with guacamole and chips also

Calories per serving: 393 / **Total Fat:** 3.4g / **Carbohydrate:** 50.5g / **Dietary Fiber:** 14.5g / **Sugars:** 7.3g / **Protein:** 21g

Chapter Six
Vegan Recipes

47. Slow-Cooker Vegan Chili (Breakfast)

Servings: 6 / **Prep. Time:** 20 min. / **Cook Time:** 4 hrs. 30 min.

Ingredients:

- 4 cups of diced butternut squash
- 1 large onion, chopped
- 1 medium red bell pepper, diced
- 4 minced cloves of garlic
- 2 cups of chicken broth
- 1 can (15 ounces) of rinsed black beans no-salt-added
- 1 can of rinsed pinto beans no-salt-added
- 1 can of petite-diced tomatoes no-salt-added
- 2 tablespoons of chili powder
- 2 tablespoons of ground cumin
- 2 teaspoons of smoked paprika
- 2 medium avocados, sliced
- For garnish chopped fresh cilantro

Instructions:

1. In a 6-quart crockpot, mix the squash, bell pepper, garlic, onion, broth, black beans, tomato, chili powder, pinto beans, cumin, paprika, and salt.
2. Cook on high for 4 hrs. or on low for 8 hrs. Mash some squash, so the broth is thickened. If desired, garnish with cilantro and serve topped with avocado.

Calories: 314 / **Total Fat:** 11.8g / **Saturated Fat:** 1.5g / **Carbohydrates:** 45.8g / **Fiber:** 15.6g / **Sugar:** 8g / **Protein**: 10.8g / **Exchange Other Carbs:** 3

48. Slow-Cooker Breakfast Beans (Breakfast)

Serves: 4 / **Prep. Time:** 30 min. / **Cook Time:** 5 hrs.

Ingredients:

- 1 tbsp. of olive oil
- 1 onion thinly sliced
- 2 garlic cloves, chopped
- 1 white/red wine vinegar
- 1 heaped tbsp. of soft brown sugar
- 400g can of pinto beans, drained and rinsed
- 200ml of passata
- Coriander small bunch, chopped

Instructions:

1. In a wide frying pan, heat the oil and fry the onion until the browning begins, then add garlic and cook for one min. Add the sugar and vinegar and bubble for a single minute. Stir in the passata and beans and season it with black pepper. Tip all of it into a Slow-Cooker.
2. Cook for 5 hours on low. Increase the heat if the sauce looks thin and cook for some more minutes. Stir the coriander into it.

Calories: 149 / **Carbs:** 21g / **Fiber:** 5g / **Sugars:** 12g / **Protein:** 6g / **Salt:** 0.39g

49. Ratatouille with Lentils (Breakfast)

Servings: 6 / **Prep. Time:** 20 min. / **Cook Time:** 4 hrs.

Ingredients:

- 1 cup of dry lentils, rinsed and drained
- 1 (12 ounces) of small eggplant, peeled and cubed
- 2 (14.5 ounces) cans of diced tomatoes with garlic, basil, and oregano, undrained
- 2 large onions, coarsely chopped
- 2 medium summer squash yellow
- 1 medium red sweet pepper
- ½ cup of water
- ¼–½ teaspoon of ground black pepper

Directions:

1. Combine the lentils, eggplant, onions, summer squash, undrained tomatoes, sweet pepper, black pepper, and water in a 3 ½–1/4-quart Slow-Cooker. Cover and simmer for 8–9 hrs. on low heat or 4 to 4 1/2 hrs. on high heat.

Calories: 215 / **Carbohydrates:** 42g / **Fiber:** 14g / **Sugar:** 1g / **Protein:** 12g

50. Fruit Compote with Ginger (Lunch)

Servings: 10 / **Prep. Time:** 15 min. / **Cook Time:** 3 hrs.

Ingredients:

- 3 medium pears, cored and cubed
- 1 can (15 ounces) of undrained pineapple chunks
- ¾ cup of quartered dried apricots
- 3 tbsp. of frozen orange juice
- 1 tbsp. of quick-cooking tapioca
- 1 tsp. of freshly grated ginger
- 1/2 tsp. of ground ginger
- 2 cups of pitted dark sweet cherries (frozen unsweetened)
- ¼ cup of toasted flaked coconut

Instructions:

1. Combine pear, orange juice, dried apricots, tapioca, undrained pineapple, and ginger in a 3 ½–¼ -quarters Slow-Cooker.
2. Cover and cook for 6-8 hours on low heat or for 3–4 hours on high-heat. In the end, stir in the cherries.
3. Spoon warm compote in dessert plates to serve—coconut topping.

Calories: 124 / **Total Fat:** 1.2g / **Saturated Fat:** 0.9g / **Carbohydrates:** 29.4g / **Fiber:** 3.5g / **Sugar:** 23g / **Protein:** 1.5g / **Exchange Other Carbs**: 2

51. Slow-Cooked Sweet and Sour Cabbage (Lunch)

Servings: 6 /**Prep. Time:** 20 mins. /**Cook Time:** 2 hrs. 30 mins.

Ingredients:

- 6 cups of shredded red cabbage
- 2 large apples
- ¼ cup of cider vinegar
- ¼ cup of water
- 3 tablespoons of dark brown sugar
- 1 tablespoon of canola oil
- 1 ½ teaspoon of crushed dried thyme
- ¼ teaspoon of salt
- ¼ teaspoon of black pepper
- ⅛ teaspoon of ground cloves

Instructions:

1. Combine the apples, vinegar, cabbage, water, brown sugar, thyme, pepper, salt, cloves, and oil into a 3 ½ or 4-quarter Slow-Cooker. Mix well.
2. Cover and simmer for 4–5 hrs. on low heat or 2 to 2 ½ hrs. on high heat. Before serving, stir.

   Calories: 90 / **Total Fat:** 2.5g / **Saturated Fat:** 0.2g / **Carbohydrates:** 17.3g / **Fiber:** 2.5g / **Sugar:** 13g / **Protein:** 1.1g / **Exchange Other Carbs:** 1

52. Slow-Cooker Burrito Bowls (Lunch)

Servings: 4 / **Prep. Time:** 10 min. / **Cook Time:** 3 hrs.

Ingredients:

- 1 diced/thinly sliced onion
- 1 diced bell pepper
- 1 finely chopped mild red chili
- 400g tin of black beans drained
- 215g of uncooked brown rice
- 400g tin of chopped tomatoes
- 150 ml (½ cup) of water
- 1 tbsp. of hot chipotle sauce
- 1 tsp. of smoked paprika
- ½ tsp. of ground cumin
- Black pepper
- Salt

Instructions:

1. Add all (not toppings) burrito bowl ingredients to a crockpot. Mix well.
2. Cook around 3 hours on low, or until cooked rice.
3. Serve hot with toppings of your choice.

Calories: 389 / **Fat:** 2.8g / **Saturated Fat:** 0.5g / **Carbohydrates:** 80.5g / **Fiber:** 8.7g / **Sugar:** 5.6g / **Protein:** 12.1g

53. Carrot Rillettes with Dukkah (Dinner)

Servings: 16 / **Prep. Time:** 30 min. / **Cook Time:** 3 hrs. 30 min.

Ingredients:

- 2 pounds of medium carrots, peeled
- 2 cups of melted coconut oil
- ½ cup of unsalted shelled pistachios
- ¼ cup of hazelnuts
- ¼ cup of unsalted sunflower seeds
- 2 tablespoons of sesame seeds
- 1 ½ teaspoon of coriander seeds
- 1 ½ teaspoon of fennel seeds
- 1 ½ teaspoon of cumin seeds
- Flaky salt 1 ¼ teaspoon
- ¾ teaspoon of ground pepper, divided
- ½ teaspoon of dried mint
- Crushed red pepper
- 2 tablespoons of cider vinegar
- 1-2 teaspoons of harissa
- 1 teaspoon of grated fresh ginger
- 1 teaspoon o kosher salt

Instructions:

1. In a 6-quart or bigger Slow-Cooker or in a wide pot, in a single layer, put the carrots. Put oil on them. Cook on high in the crockpot or cover it and bake in an oven of 250°F until the carrots are fully tender, 3–4 hours.
2. Meanwhile, at med-low heat in a med skillet, toast pistachios, hazelnuts, sesame seeds and, sunflower seeds stirring continuously, until fragrant, for 2–4 min. To a bowl, transfer it.
3. Enhances heat to med-high. Add the coriander, cumin seeds, and fennel to the pan and toast for around 30 secs, stirring the pan till fragrant. Move to a clean spice grinder or mortar and pestle and grind firmly.
4. To the food processor, move the nut mixture, then pulse till finely chopped. Return with the flaky salt, toasted spices, 1/2 teaspoon pepper, crushed red pepper, and mint back to the bowl; combine well.
5. Transfer the carrots to a food processor using tongs. In addition to vinegar, ginger, kosher salt, harissa to taste, and the rest ¼ tbsp. of pepper, add 1 tbsp. of still warm oil.
6. ¼ cups of a serving tray, arrange the rillettes, and sprinkle it with dukkah.

Calories: 75 / **Total Fat:** 5.5g / **Saturated Fat:** 3.6g / **Carbohydrates:** 6g / **Fiber:** 1.9g / **Sugar:** 3g / **Protein:** 0.9g

54. Vegan Jambalaya Slow-Cooker (Dinner)

Servings: 6–8 / **Prep. Time:** 10 min. / **Cook Time:** 6 hrs.

Ingredients:

- 1 tbsp. of olive oil
- 1 diced green bell pepper
- 2 diced celery stalks
- 1 diced medium onion
- 3 garlic cloves minced
- 1 ½ cups of diced tomatoes (about 3 tomatoes)
- 4–5 cups of vegetable broth
- 2 tbsp. of paprika
- 2 tbsp. of ground cumin
- 2 tsp. of ground black pepper
- 1 tsp. of dried thyme
- 1 tsp. of dried oregano
- 2 tbsp. of cayenne pepper
- 2 cups of brown rice long grain
- 1 ¾ cups (1 14 oz. can) of drained red kidney beans cooked
- 2 cups of chopped vegan sausage (optional)
- 2–3 scallions chopped

Instructions:

Put the oil, the pepper, the celery, the onion, the garlic, the tomatoes, the four cups of broth, the paprika, the cumin, the black pepper, the thyme, the oregano, and the hot sauce in a low-heat Slow-Cooker.

1. Cover, stirring regularly, and cook for 4 to 5 hours.
2. Increase the heat to high levels but first Add the rice.
3. For an additional hour, then a further half-hour, mix, cover and simmer, stirring regularly, until the rice is tender, all the liquid is absorbed if the rice gets too dry during preparation, add more broth.
4. Add the sausage and beans. Cook and stir for another 2 mins. or so, before both the sausage and beans are cooked.
5. Served with scallions on top.

Calories: 383 / **Fat:** 6.2g / **Saturated Fat:** 1.1g / **Carbohydrates:** 69.6g / **Fiber:** 9.1g / **Sugar:** 5.4g / **Protein:** 13.8g

55. Slow-Cooker Moroccan Chickpea Stew (Dinner)

Servings: 6/ **Prep. Time:** 10 min. / **Cook Time:** 4 hrs.

Ingredients:

- 1 medium white onion chopped
- 3 minced garlic cloves
- 1 small butternut squash peeled and chopped
- 1 chopped red bell pepper
- ¾ cup of red lentils
- 1 (15oz.) can of drained and rinsed chickpeas
- 1 (15oz.) can pure tomato sauce
- 1 teaspoon of freshly grated ginger
- 1 teaspoon of turmeric
- 1 teaspoon of cumin
- 1 teaspoon of smoked paprika
- ½ teaspoon of cinnamon
- 1/2 teaspoon of salt and pepper
- 3 cups of vegetable broth

Instructions:

1. Use a Slow-Cooker to add all the ingredients. Stir to mix, then cover and simmer for 3–4 hours on high (or on low 6–7 hours.)
2. Take the cover off for a thicker stew with 1 hour remaining in the cooking process.
3. Serve with arugula, yogurt, and quinoa.

Calories: 178 / **Carbohydrates:** 37g / **Protein:** 8g / **Fiber:** 11g / **Sugar:** 8g

56. Vegan Keto Walnut Chili (Dinner)

Servings: 6 to 8/ **Prep. Time:** 10 min. / **Cook Time:** 31 mins.

Ingredients:

- 2 tbsp. of extra virgin olive oil
- 5 celery stalks finely diced
- 2 minced cloves garlic
- 1 ½ tsp. of ground cinnamon
- 2 tsp. of chili powder
- 4 tsp. of ground cumin
- 1 ½ tsp. of smoked paprika
- 2 peppers large chipotle in adobo, minced
- 2 green bell peppers finely diced
- 2 zucchini, diced
- 8oz. of cremini mushrooms, minced
- 1 ½ tbsp of tomato paste
- 1 (15oz.) can of diced tomatoes
- 3 cups of water
- ½ cup of coconut milk
- 2 ½ cups of soy meat crumbled
- 1 cup of raw walnuts minced
- 1 tbsp. of unsweetened cocoa powder
- Salt and pepper

To serve:

- 2 tbsp. of Fresh cilantro leaves
- 1 Avocado, sliced
- 2 tbsp. of Sliced radishes

Instructions:

1. Over medium heat, in a big pot, heat the oil. Add the celery then cook for 4 mins. Add the garlic, chili powder, cinnamon, paprika, and cumin and mix for another 2mins., until fragrant.

2. Add the mushrooms, bell peppers, and zucchini and cook for 5mins.

3. Add the chipotle, tomatoes, tomato paste, coconut milk, water, soy meat, cocoa powder, and walnuts. Lower the heat to med-low and simmer until thick, and the veggies are soft for around 20–25 minutes.

4. Season with pepper and salt. Avocado, cilantro, and radishes on top.

Calories: 353 / **Fat:** 28g / **Saturated Fat:** 6g / **Carbohydrates:** 18g / **Fiber:** 8g / **Sugar:** 5g / **Protein:** 13g

Chapter Seven
Fish and Seafood

57. Slow-Cooker Fish and Tomatoes (Low-Carb, Paleo, Whole30)

Servings: 4 / **Prep. Time:** 10 min. / **Cook Time:** 2 hrs. 30 min.

Ingredients:

- 1 lb. of fish
- 1 diced bell pepper
- 1 diced small onion
- 1 minced garlic cloves
- 15 ounces of diced tomatoes
- 1 tsp. of dried herbs
- 1/3 cup of low-sodium broth (vegetable/chicken)
- ½ tsp. of salt
- 1/4 tsp. of pepper

Instructions:

1. To the Slow-Cooker, add onion, broth, tomatoes, bell pepper, and garlic. Stir well.

2. Add fish on the top of the mixture of tomato. Sprinkle the fish with salt, herbs, and pepper. Pour the broth over the top.

3. Cook 1–2hrs. high or 2–4hrs.

Calories: 152 / **Total Fat:** 2.7g / **Saturated Fat:** 0.8g / **Total Carbohydrate:** 8g / **Dietary Fiber:** 1.3g / **Sugars:** 4.5g / **Protein:** 25.2g

58. Slow-Cooker Fish Fillets

Servings: 3 / **Prep. Time:** 10 min. / **Cook Time:** 3 hrs. 30 min.

Ingredients:

- 1 lb. of firm fish fillet
- Salt and pepper

Seasonings:

- Lemon slices, fresh herb, white wine
- Minced ginger, minced garlic, soy sauce
- Minced garlic, ponzu, black bean sauce
- Pesto sauce

Instructions:

1. Many fish you can use, per serving around 6 ounces, (and will fit in the crockpot). Prefer to create a whole 1 lb. fillet, but you can cook individual parts as well.
2. Put a fillet on a half piece of broad aluminum foil.
3. Season the fillet- bay leaves (fresh) with thin lemon slices and a drop of white wine are our preference. The seasonings are guidelines. Use your idea.
4. Turn the foil back, roll the edges up and seal tightly. That holds the juices within, removing the need for washing. If it does escape, it is always easy to clean up.
5. Set aside in a Slow-Cooker.
6. Cook for 3 hours on low.
7. From the cooker remove and open carefully, steam can come out.

Calories: 158.7 / **Total Fat:** 1.3g / **Saturated Fat:** 0.2g / **Total Carbohydrate:** 0g / **Dietary Fiber:** 0g / **Sugars:** 0g / **Protein:** 34.5g

59. Keto Slow-Cooker Tilapia

Servings: 2 / **Prep. Time:** 3 min. / **Cook Time:** 1 hr. 30 min.

Ingredients:

- 4 tilapia fillets
- 1 lemon
- 2 tablespoons of unsalted butter
- ½ teaspoon of salt
- Pepper

Instructions:

1. Place the tilapia on the Slow-Cooker's bottom. Add butter over the top and lemon slices. Close the cover, then scheduled for one hour and 30 mins.

Calories: 549 / **Total Fat:** 21g / **Saturated Fat:** 10g / **Carbohydrates:** 4g / **Fiber:** 1g / **Sugar:** 1g / **Protein:** 90g

60. Slow-Cooker Seafood Stew Recipe

Servings: 6 / **Prep. Time:** 15 min. / **Cook Time:** 3 hrs. 30 min.

Ingredients:

- 28 ounces of can crushed tomatoes
- 1 tablespoon of tomato paste
- 4 cups of vegetable broth
- 3 minced garlic cloves
- 1 pound of yellow potatoes
- ½ cup of chopped white onion
- 1 teaspoon of dried thyme
- 1 teaspoon of dried basil
- 1 teaspoon of dried oregano
- ½ teaspoon of celery salt
- ¼ teaspoon of red pepper flakes crushed
- 1/8 teaspoon of cayenne pepper
- Salt and pepper
- 2 pounds of seafood
- Chopped parsley handful

Instructions:

1. In a Slow-Cooker, mix all the ingredients except seafood. Cover and simmer for 2 to 3 hours on high or 4 to 6 hours at low before the potatoes are cooked.
2. To the Slow-Cooker, add thawed seafood and move to high heat. Cook for 30–60min., till thoroughly cooked seafood.
3. Parsley for garnish.
4. Serve hot.

Calories: 111 / **Carbohydrates:** 19g / **Protein:** 6g / **Fat:** 1g / **Fiber:** 4g / **Sugar:** 5g

61. Seafood Cioppino

Servings: 8 / **Prep. Time:** 20 min. / **Cook Time:** 4 hrs. 30 min.

Ingredients:

- 1 can (28 ounces) of diced tomatoes
- 2 medium onions, chopped
- 3 celery ribs, chopped
- 1 bottle of clam juice
- 1 can of tomato paste
- 1/2 cup of white wine or vegetable broth
- 5 minced garlic cloves
- 1 tablespoon of red wine vinegar
- 1 tablespoon of olive oil
- 1-2 teaspoons of Italian seasoning
- 1 bay leaf
- ½ teaspoon of sugar
- 1 pound of haddock fillets
- 1 pound of uncooked shrimp (41 to 50 per pound)
- 1 can (6 ounces) of chopped clams, undrained
- 1 can (6 ounces) of lump crabmeat, drained
- 2 tablespoons of minced fresh parsley

Instructions:

1. In the Slow-Cooker (4-/5-qt.) first 12 ingredients are combined. Cook, sealed, 4–5 hours on low.
2. Stir the seafood in. Cook until the fish starts flaking comfortably with a fork, and shrimp turns pink for 20–30 mins.
3. Removing the bay leaves.
4. Stir the parsley.

Calories: 205 / **Fat:** 3g / **Saturated Fat:** 1 / **Cholesterol:** 125mg / **Carbohydrate:** 15g / **Sugars:** 8g / **Fiber:** 3g / **Protein:** 29g

62. Slow-Cooker Shrimp Boil

Servings: 6 / **Prep. Time:** 15 min. / **Cook Time:** 5 hrs.

Ingredients:

- ¼ cup of seafood seasoning, (old bay)
- 2 large ears of yellow corn
- 1 1/2 pounds of large, deveined, shell-on shrimp
- 8 ounces of kielbasa
- 3 cloves of garlic, lightly smashed
- 2 bay leaves
- 2 medium yellow onions
- ½ cup of chopped fresh parsley
- ¼ cup of fresh lemon juice
- Crusty bread
- 3 pounds of red bliss potatoes

Instructions:

1. Place the potatoes, garlic, onions, two tbsp of seafood seasoning, bay leaves, and 4 cups of water in a 6-quarter crockpot. Stir to blend. Cover with a lid, then cook for 4 hours on low heat.
2. Remove the lid off and change to high heat. Stir softly in the corn, sausage, shrimp, and the seafood two more tablespoons of seasoning. Cover with a lid and cook for 30 to 45min., before the shrimp becomes opaque and sausage gets warm. Stir in the lemon juice and the parsley gently.
3. Serve straight from the Slow-Cooker, or place in a wide serving bowl and serve with crusty bread immediately.

Calories: 490 / **Fat:** 20.5g / **Saturated:** 6.2g / **Carbs:** 33.0g / **Fiber:** 3.9g / **Sugars:** 4.9g / **Protein:** 46.4g

63. Crockpot New Orleans Spicy Barbecue Shrimp Recipe

Servings: 4 / **Prep. Time:** 15 min. / **Cook Time:** 1 hr.

Ingredients:

- 2 garlic cloves minced
- 1 tsp. of Cajun seasoning
- ½ cup of unsalted butter
- ¼ cup of Worcestershire sauce
- 1 tbsp. of hot pepper sauce
- 1 lemon juice
- Salt and pepper
- 1 ½ pound of large shrimp unpeeled
- 1 finely chopped green onion

Instructions:

1. In the crockpot, mix the garlic, Cajun seasoning, lemon juice, butter, hot pepper, and Worcestershire sauce. Season with salt and pepper. Cover and simmer for 30min. or until warm.
2. Rinse and drain the shrimp.
3. ½ spoon of the crockpot sauce in a measuring cup.
4. Place the shrimp in the Slow-Cooker and with the remaining sauce drizzle.
5. To coat equally, stir it.
6. Cover and cook on high till opaque are the shrimps.
7. Sprinkle green onion and serve warm.

Calories: 400 / **Fat:** 25g / **Saturated Fat:** 15g / **Carbohydrates:** 7g / **Fiber:** 1g / **Sugar:** 3g / **Protein:** 36g

64. Slow-Cooker Maple Salmon

Servings: 6/**Prep. Time:** 10 min./**Cook Time:** 2 hrs.

Ingredients:

- 6 salmon fillets (fresh or frozen)
- ½ cup of maple syrup
- 1/8 cup of lime juice
- ¼ cup of soy sauce
- 2 tsp. of crushed garlic
- 1 tsp. of minced ginger root

Instructions:

1. Place pieces of salmon in a Slow-Cooker (3 ½ quarts).
2. Combine the ingredients of the sauce and add salmon over them.
3. On high, cover, and crock.

Calories: 426 / **Carbohydrates:** 14.7g / **Protein:** 40.1g / **Fat:** 22g / **Saturated Fat:** 4.5g / **Sugar:** 11.6g

65. Slow-Cooker Cajun Corn and Shrimp Chowder

Servings: 4 / **Prep. Time:** 10 min. / **Cook Time:** 5 hrs.

Ingredients:

- 16 oz. of frozen sweet corn
- ½ pound of red baby potatoes
- ¼ cup of flour
- 1 ½ teaspoon of Cajun seasoning
- 4 cups of chicken broth
- ½ cup of heavy cream
- 12 oz. of shrimp
- Salt and pepper

Instructions:

1. Clean and dice potatoes into chunks of bite-size.
2. In a Slow-Cooker, add corn and potatoes and cover with flour.
3. Add the broth and Cajun seasoning.
4. Cover and cook for 2 to 3 hours on high, or 4 to 6 hours on low.
5. Change to high the Slow-Cooker.
6. Add shrimp and cream.
7. Cook for a further 30–60 minutes until shrimp are pink and cooked.
8. Garnish with salt and pepper and serve.

Calories: 406 / **Carbohydrates:** 45g / **Protein:** 28g / **Fat:** 14g / **Saturated Fat:** 7g / **Fiber:** 4g / **Sugar:** 1g

66. Low Cooker/Instant Pot Coconut Curry Shrimp (Low-Carb, Paleo, Whole30)

Servings: 4 / **Prep. Time:** 5 min. / **Cook Time:** 2 hrs.

Ingredients:

- 1 pound of shrimp
- 30 ounces of coconut milk
- 2 minced garlic cloves
- 1 tablespoon of yellow curry powder
- 1 teaspoon of salt
- 1 lime juice
- ¼ cup chopped fresh cilantro, (optional)

Instructions:

1. Use the Slow-Cooker to add curry powder, coconut milk, salt, lime juice, and garlic. Stir well.
2. Cook for 1–2 hours on high or 3–4 on low.
3. Add shrimp and cook for another 15–30 minutes, or until shrimp is done. Top with cilantro.

Calories Per Serving: 204 / **Saturated Fat:** 8.1g / **Total Carbohydrate:** 3.3g / **Dietary Fiber:** 0.5g / **Sugar:** 1.4g / **Protein:** 24.2g

67. Crockpot Shrimp and Grits Recipe

Servings: 6 / **Prep. Time:** 10 min. / **Cook Time:** 6 hrs.

Ingredients:

- 2 cups of grits
- Salt and pepper
- ¼ cup of heavy cream
- 1 cup of shredded cheese
- 2 tbsp. of butter unsalted
- 2 tsp. of hot sauce
- 1 pound of shrimp cooked, peeled, deveined
- 1 tbsp. of chives chopped

Instructions:

1. In a Slow-Cooker, mix grits, water (8 cups), 1 1/2 tsp. of salt, and whisk together.
2. Cover and cook for 6 hours on low until liquid is absorbed.
3. Mix in cream, butter, cheese, and hot sauce. Stir until the cheese melts.
4. Season to the required flavor with salt and pepper.
5. Put on top, the shrimps. Cover and cook until the shrimp is warmed up, around 5mins.
6. Serving with chives. **Calories:** 393 / **Fat:** 13g / **Saturated Fat:** 7g / **Carbohydrates:** 42g / **Fiber:** 1g / **Sugar:** 1g / **Protein:** 24g

68. Crockpot Low Country Boil

Servings: 6 / **Prep. Time:** 10min. / **Cook Time:** 7 hrs. 40min.

Ingredients:

- 1.5 lbs. of small red potatoes, cut in half
- 5 cups of water
- 1 bottle (12 oz.) of beer (you can also sub in broth)
- ¼ cup of old bay seasoning
- 2 stalks celery
- 1 onion
- 3–4 garlic cloves minced
- 2 lemons
- 1 lb. of cooked kielbasa sausage
- 4 fresh corn cobs
- 2 lb. of uncooked fresh large shrimp

Instructions:

1. Start by adding cooking spray on a Slow-Cooker (6 or 7 quarts). Add water, liquor, garlic, and Old Bay Seasoning. Stir until blended properly.
2. In a Slow-Cooker, put the potatoes, celery, and onion and squeeze the lemons over the mixture.
3. To a Slow-Cooker, put the lemon halves.
4. Cover the crockpot, then simmer for 4–5 hours on low heat.
5. Attach corn and sausage, cover, and cook two hours longer.
6. Increase to high the heat setting and add your shrimp to it. Your crockpot is going to be full. Do the best to mix a bit and squeeze the shrimp and cook after covering for 30–40 mins. or until the shrimp is pink.
7. Drain the low country boil crockpot using a broad strainer. Serve this meal for quick cleaning on a table. Enjoy it with cocktail sauce, lemon, and some seasoning like Cajun.

Calories: 444 / **Carbohydrates:** 49g / **Protein:** 18g / **Fat:** 22g / **Saturated Fat:** 7g / **Fiber:** 15g / **Sugar:** 3g

69. Slow-Cooker Fish Au Gratin

Servings: 6 / **Prep. Time:** 10 min. / **Cook Time:** 2 hrs.

Ingredients:

- 6 tablespoons of butter
- 3 tablespoons of flour
- 1 ½ teaspoon of salt
- ½ tablespoon of dry mustard
- ¼ tablespoon of ground nutmeg
- 1 ¼ cup of milk
- 1 ½ teaspoon of lemon juice
- 1 cup of shredded cheddar cheese
- Whitefish fillets frozen 3 pounds, thawed

Instructions:

1. Over medium heat, put the butter in a med saucepan and mix until melted. Add the flour, salt, nutmeg, and dry mustard and mix until smooth. Let it simmer, stirring regularly, for a few minutes.
2. Stir in the milk gently and stir vigorously till the mixture becomes dense. Lemon juice and cheese are added. Until the cheese has melted, stir on medium heat.
3. The fish is placed on the crockpot bottom. To cover it, spill the cheese sauce uniformly over the fish top.
4. Cover the Slow-Cooker and simmer for 1 ½ hour on high or until the fish quickly flakes with a fork. Serve it hot.

Calories: 413 / **Fat:** 21g / **Carbohydrates:** 6g / **Protein:** 47g

70. Low-Cooker Tuna Noodle Casserole

Servings: 10 / **Prep. Time:** 25 min. / **Cook Time:** 4hrs.

Ingredients:

- ¼ cup of butter cubed
- ½ pound of sliced fresh mushrooms
- 1 chopped medium onion
- 1 chopped medium sweet pepper
- 1 teaspoon of salt
- 1 teaspoon of pepper
- 2 minced garlic cloves
- ¼ cup of all-purpose flour
- 2 cups of chicken broth reduced sodium
- 2 cups of half-and-half cream

Instructions:

1. Melt butter over med-high heat in a wide skillet. Add the mushrooms, onion, ½ teaspoon of salt, sweet pepper, and ½ tsp. of pepper; cook and mix for 6–8 mins., until soft. Include garlic, and simmer for 1 minute. Add flour until mixed. In broth, whisk gradually. Bring to boil, stirring frequently; simmer for 1–2 minutes and stir until thickened.
2. Transfer to Slow-Cooker (5-qt.). Add cream. Cook 4–5 hours, covered, at low till noodles are tender. In the meantime, add the tuna, remaining salt and pepper, and lemon juice in a shallow bowl.
3. Remove from the Slow-Cooker. In a noodle mixture, stir in cheese, peas, and tuna mixture. Let uncovered stand for 20 minutes. Sprinkle with potato chips right before serving.

Calories: 393 / **Fat:** 21g / **Saturated Fat:** 12g / **Cholesterol:** 84mg / **Carbohydrate**: 28g / **Sugars:** 5g / **Fiber:** 3g / **Protein:** 22g

71. Crock-Pot Crab Rangoon Dip Recipe

Servings: 8 / **Prep. Time:** 10min. / **Cook Time:** 2 hrs.

Ingredients:

- 16 ounces of softened cream cheese
- ½ cup of sour cream
- 4 whole chopped green onions
- 1 ½ teaspoon of Worcestershire sauce
- ½ teaspoon of garlic powder
- 12 ounces of shredded crab meat

Instructions:

1. Add all the ingredients to a Slow-Cooker (2.5-3 quart) and mix to combine.

2. Cover and simmer for 2 hours on low, stirring every 30 mins. to ensure that the cream cheese is evenly melted.

3. To warm setting, turn Slow-Cooker, and put chips, crackers, or fried wonton skins to serve.

Calories: 251 / **Total Fat:** 18g / **Saturated Fat:** 12g / **Carbohydrates:** 11g / **Dietary Fiber:** 0.2g / **Sugars:** 6g / **Protein:** 8g

Chapter Eight
Soup and Stew Recipes

72. Slow-Cooker Low-carb Zuppa Toscana Soup

Servings: 8 / **Preparation Time:** 10min. / **Cook Time:** 4 hrs.

Ingredients:

- 1 lb. of Italian ground sausage mild/hot
- 1 tbsp. of oil
- ½ cup of finely diced onion (1 medium onion)
- 3 minced garlic cloves
- 36 oz. of chicken/vegetable stock
- 1 large cauliflower head, diced in small florets
- 3 cups of chopped kale
- ¼ tsp. of crushed red pepper flakes
- 1 tsp. of salt
- ½ tsp. of pepper
- ½ cup of heavy cream

Instructions:

1. Over med heat in a skillet, brown the ground sausage until done.
2. Remove the sausage using a slotted spoon and put it in a 6-quart Slow-Cooker. Take off the grease.
3. In the same skillet, put the oil and sauté onions for 3 to 4mins. until its translucent.
4. Add the Slow-Cooker with the onions, chicken/vegetable stock, cauliflower florets, red pepper flakes crushed, salt, pepper, and kale. When mixed, blend.
5. Cook for 4 hours on high, or 8 hours on low.
6. Add heavy cream and stir until mixed.

Calories: 215 / **Fat:** 16.2g / **Carbohydrates:** 6.4g / **Fiber:** 2g / **Sugar:** 3.4g / **Protein:** 10.1g

73. Garden Tomato Soup

Servings: 9 / **Prep. Time:** 15 min. / **Cook Time:** 3 hrs.

Ingredients:

- 2 pounds of Roma tomatoes chopped
- 1 (32 ounces) carton of unsalted vegetable stock
- 2 cups of assorted vegetables finely chopped (like carrot, celery, fennel, sweet pepper, onion)
- 1 (6 ounces) can of tomato paste no-salt-added
- 1 teaspoon of granulated sugar
- ¼ teaspoon of salt

Instructions:

1. Mix the tomatoes, vegetable stock, tomato paste, sugar, and salt in a Slow-Cooker (3 ½–¼ quart).
2. Cover and simmer for 6–8 hours on low heat or 3 to 4 hrs. on high.

Calories: 62 / **Total Fat:** 1g / **Saturated Fat:** 1g / **Carbohydrates:** 11g / **Fiber:** 2g / **Sugar:** 6g / **Protein:** 2g / **Exchange Other Carbs:** 1

74. Slow-Cooker Curried Butternut Squash Soup

Servings: 8 / **Prep. Time:** 10 min. / **Cook Time:** 3 hrs. 30 min.

Ingredients:

- 1 (5 cups) medium butternut squash (2–2 ½ pounds), seeded, peeled, and cubed
- 3 cups of "no-chicken" broth/vegetable broth
- 1 chopped medium onion
- 4 teaspoons of curry powder
- ½ teaspoon of garlic powder
- ¾ teaspoon of salt
- 1 (14 ounces) can of coconut milk
- 1–2 tablespoons of lime juice, plus wedges for serving
- Fresh cilantro chopped for garnish

Instructions:

1. In a Slow-Cooker (5 quarts), add squash, broth, curry powder, onion, garlic powder, and salt. Cover and simmer on low for 7 hours or high 3 ½ hours until the vegetables are really soft. Turn the heat off and whisk to taste in the coconut milk and lime juice. Puree until smooth, using an immersion blender. Cover with cilantro.

Calories: 153 / **Total Fat:** 10.8g / **Saturated Fat:** 9.4g / **Carbohydrates:** 14.5g / **Fiber:** 3.1g / **Protein:** 2.2g / **Exchange Other Carbs:** 1

75. Crock-Pot Chicken Soup (Low-Carb + Keto)

Servings: 6 / **Prep. Time:** 5 min. / **Cook Time:** 4 hrs.

Ingredients:

- 1 ½ pound of boneless/skinless bits of chicken
- 15.5 ounces of Chunky-salsa
- 15 ounces of chicken bone broth
- 8 ounces of Monterey/Pepper Jack-cheese, in small shredded cubes

Instructions:

1. Place pieces of chicken on the base of a crockpot (6 quarts).
2. Add leftover ingredients.
3. Cook 3–4 hours at high or 6–8 hours on low.
4. Remove pieces of chicken, then shred it. Return to crock.
5. Serve warm.

Net Carbs: 4g / **Calories:** 331 / **Carbs:** 5g / **Protein:** 25g / **Fat:** 23g / **Saturated Fat:** 10g / **Fiber:** 1g / **Sugar:** 3g

76. Slow-Cooker Vegetable Soup

Servings: 8 / **Prep. Time:** 10 min. / **Cook Time:** 6 hrs.

Ingredients:

- 2 tablespoons of olive oil
- 1 yellow diced onion
- 4 carrots, peeled and sliced in rounds
- 3 sliced celery ribs
- 4 minced cloves garlic
- ¼ cup of chopped fresh parsley
- 28 ounces can of diced tomatoes, undrained
- 3 cups of diced potatoes
- 2 cups of frozen/fresh green beans, ends chopped and trimmed
- 2 tablespoons of tomato paste
- 2 bay leaves
- 1 teaspoon of smoked paprika
- 3/4 teaspoon of salt
- ½ teaspoon of dried thyme
- ½ teaspoon of dried basil
- ½ teaspoon of dried oregano
- 1/4 teaspoon of fresh ground pepper, or to taste
- 8 cups of vegetable broth low-sodium
- 1 cup of frozen/fresh corn kernels
- Finely chopped dill or parsley for garnish
- For serving, fresh lemon juic

Instructions:

1. Heat the olive oil over medium to high heat in a large skillet.
2. Add the onions, celery, and carrots; cook for 4 min.
3. Add fresh parsley and garlic and cook for 30 secs.
4. Remove from the heat and transfer to your Slow-Cooker 6-quart or larger.
5. Add diced tomatoes, green beans, potatoes, tomato paste, bay leaves, salt, thyme, smoked paprika, basil, oregano, vegetable broth, and pepper to the Slow-Cooker; stir gently until all combine well.
6. Cover and cook for 6 hours on low or 3 hours on high.
7. During the last 30 mins. of cooking, add corn.
8. Fresh dill or parsley garnish in cups, with a squeeze of lemon juice (fresh lemon).
9. Serve.

Calories: 181 / **Fat:** 6g / **Saturated Fat:** 1g / **Carbohydrates:** 28g / **Fiber:** 5g / **Sugar:** 7g / **Protein:** 9g

77. Slow-Cooker Mediterranean Stew

Servings: 6 / **Prep. Time:** 15 min. / **Cook Time:** 6 hrs. 30 min.

Ingredients:

- 2 (14 ounces) cans of fire-roasted diced tomatoes no-salt-added
- 3 cups of vegetable broth low-sodium
- 1 cup of coarsely chopped onion
- ¾ cup of chopped carrot
- 4 minced cloves garlic
- 1 teaspoon of dried oregano
- ¾ teaspoon of salt
- ½ teaspoon of crushed red pepper
- ¼ teaspoon of ground pepper
- 1 (15 ounces) can of chickpeas no-salt-added, divided rinsed
- 1 bunch lacinato kale, chopped and stemmed (8 cups)
- 1 tablespoon of lemon juice
- 3 tablespoons of olive oil extra-virgin
- Fresh basil leaves
- 6 lemon wedges (optional)

Instructions:

1. In a Slow-Cooker (6-quart), mix the tomato, onion, carrot, broth, garlic, salt, oregano, red pepper crushed, and pepper. Cover and simmer for 6 hours on low.
2. Measure cooking liquid ¼ cup from the crockpot in a small bowl. Add 2 tbsp. of chickpeas: mash until smooth with a fork.
3. In the crockpot, add mashed chickpea, lemon juice, kale, and leftover whole chickpea to the mix. To combine, stir. Cover and simmer for about 30 minutes on low, until the kale is soft.
4. Ladle the stew into six bowls evenly: drizzle with the oil. Add basil to garnish. When needed, serve with lemon wedges.

Calories: 191 / **Total Fat:** 7.8g / **Saturated Fat:** 1g / **Carbohydrates:** 22.9g / **Fiber:** 5.6g / **Sugar:** 7g / **Protein:** 5.7g / **Exchange Other Carbs:** 2

78. Slow-Cooker Vegetable and Tofu Thai Stew

Servings: 5 / **Prep. Time:** 20 min. / **Cook Time:** 4 hrs. 15 min.

Ingredients:

- 1 (13.5 ounces) can of light coconut milk
- 1 cup of water
- 3 tablespoons of red curry pastes
- 3 (1 tablespoon) finely chopped garlic cloves
- 2 teaspoons of finely chopped lemongrass
- 10 ounces (about 2 ½ cups) of small cauliflower florets
- 3 (2 cups) peeled small carrots, cut diagonally in ¼" thick slices
- 1 (1 ½ cups) medium red onion, cut in ½" wedges
- 1 (2 cups) medium zucchini, cut in half and in ½" thick slices
- 1 (14 ounces) extra-firm tofu package, drained
- 1 tablespoon of canola oil
- 1 tablespoon of light brown sugar
- ¼ teaspoon of kosher salt
- ¼ cup of fresh cilantro leaves
- 2 tablespoons of roasted chopped unsalted peanuts

Instructions:

1. In a 5–6-quart Slow-Cooker, mix the coconut milk, red curry paste, water, lemongrass, and garlic until smooth. Stir in carrots, onions, and cauliflower. Cover and cook around 4 hours on low, until the vegetables are soft. To the Slow-Cooker, add the zucchini; cover and cook till the zucchini is soft, around 15 mins.
2. Meanwhile, slice the tofu into 1" pieces. Use a paper towel to pat these cubes dry. Steam up the oil over med-high in a wide skillet. Add tofu to the pan and cook for 8–10 mins. on both sides till deep brown, frequently rotating equally to cooked both sides. In a Slow-Cooker, stir the brown sugar, tofu, and salt. Ladle stew in the bowl; cover with the peanuts and the cilantro.

Calories: 243 / **Total Fat:** 14g / **Saturated Fat:** 5g / **Carbohydrates:** 20g / **Fiber:** 4g / **Sugar:** 9g / **Protein:** 12g / **Exchange Other Carbs:** 2

79. Slow-Cooker Vegetable Stew

Servings: 6 / **Prep. Time:** 35 min. / **Cook Time:** 8 hrs. 20 min.

Ingredients:

- 1 (28 ounces) can of whole plum tomatoes
- 1 (15 ounces) can of cannellini beans rinsed
- 1 ½ cups of Italian (romano) beans frozen cut
- 12 ounces of baby yellow potatoes
- 1 cup of chopped onion
- 2 teaspoons of dried oregano
- 1 teaspoon of salt
- ½ teaspoon of ground pepper
- ½ teaspoon of crushed red pepper, more for serving
- 1 cup of no-chicken broth/vegetable broth low-sodium
- 1 tablespoon of extra-virgin olive oil
- 3 minced cloves of garlic
- For garnish, shaved parmesan cheese

Instructions:

1. In a 4–7-quart Slow-Cooker, put the tomatoes and its juice and smash them with the hands or with a potato masher. Add the cannellini, the frozen beans, the potatoes, the onion, the oregano, the salt, the pepper, and the crushed red pepper. Stir the broth, then cover. Cook for 8 hours on low or 4 hours on high.
2. To cook the croutons, preheat the oven to 400°F for approximately 30mins. before eating. Mash the garlic with a fork or side of a chef's knife into a paste. Move to a med bowl and whisk in the oil and 2 tablespoons of Italian seasoning. Add the bread to coat and toss. Move to a baking sheet in a rimmed shape. Bake for 12 to 15 minutes until it is golden.
3. Before serving, heat 1 tablespoon of oil over med heat in a small skillet. Add minced garlic, then cook for around 1 minute, stirring, until golden. In the crockpot, stir in garlic and oil. Split the stew into 6 bowls, then finish with the croutons. Serve with other crushed red pepper, and if needed, parmesan.

Calories: 407 / **Total Fat:** 10.9 / **Saturated Fat:** 1.6g / **Carbohydrates:** 62.8g / **Fiber:** 12.4g / **Sugar:** 11g / **Protein:** 16g / **Exchange Other Carbs:** 4

80. Southwestern Sweet Potato Stew

Servings: 6 / **Prep. Time:** 15 min. / **Cook Time:** 10 hrs.

Ingredients:

- 2 cups of vegetable broth lower-sodium
- 2 cups of water
- 1 ½ pound of sweet potatoes, and cut into 2" pieces, peeled
- 1 (½ cup) chopped medium onion
- 2 minced cloves of garlic
- 1 ½ teaspoon of crushed dried oregano
- 1 teaspoon of chili powder
- ½ teaspoon of ground cumin
- ¼ teaspoon of salt
- 1 (15 ounces) can of golden hominy, drained and rinsed
- 1 (15 ounces) can of black beans no-salt-added, drained and rinsed
- 1 roasted poblano chile pepper, cut into thin strips seeds and removed
- Fresh cilantro chopped
- Lime wedges

Instructions:

1. In a 3 ½–¼ -quart Slow-Cooker, mix the vegetable broth, water, onion, garlic, oregano, sweet potatoes, chili powder, cumin, and salt. Add the beans, poblano pepper, and hominy.
2. Cover and cook for 10–12 hours on low.
3. Mash sweet potatoes coarsely with a masher, sprinkle the cilantro, and finally, use lime wedges to serve.

Calories: 202 / **Total Fat:** 0.9g / **Saturated Fat:** 0.1g / **Carbohydrates:** 42.1g / **Fiber:** 8.5g / **Sugar:** 5g / **Protein:** 6.9g / **Exchange Other Carbs:** 3

81. Low-Carb Beef Cabbage Stew

Servings: 8 / **Prep. time:** 15 min. / **Cook Time:** 2 hrs. 5 min.

Ingredients:

- 2 pounds of beef stew meat, (trimmed and cut into 1-inch cubes)
- 1 cube of beef-bouillon
- 1 ⅓ cups of chicken-broth (hot)
- 2 large onions, (coarsely chopped)
- 1 tsp. of greek-seasoning
- ¼ tsp. of ground black pepper
- 2 bay leaves
- 1 (8 ounces) package of shredded-cabbage
- 5 celery stalks, sliced
- 1 (8 ounces) can of whole plum tomatoes (coarsely chopped)
- 1 (8 ounces) can of tomato sauce
- 1 pinch of salt to taste

Instructions:

1. In a large saucepan/Dutch oven, cook and stir the beef until browned, around 5 minutes; remove the excess of grease.
2. In a bowl, stir the beef bouillon in the chicken broth until dissolved; add to the beef.
3. Mix the onions, pepper, bay leaves, and Greek-seasoning in the broth-beef; cover the saucepan and simmer for around 1 hour and 15 minutes until the beef is tender. Add the broth-beef mixture with the celery and cabbage; cover the saucepan and cook about 30 more minutes until the celery is tender.
4. Stir in broth-beef mixture with tomato sauce, plum tomatoes, and salt, then simmer until stew is slightly thickened, for 15–20 minutes, before serving. Remove the bay leaves.

Net Carbs: 9g / **Cal:** 372.1 / **Protein:** 31.7g / **Fat:** 23g / **Cholesterol:** 100mg

Keto Slow Cooker Cookbook

Chapter Nine
Rice Recipes

82. Keto Crockpot Jambalaya

Servings: 8 / **Prep. Time:** 15 min. / **Cook Time:** 6 hrs.

Ingredients: Calories: 253 / **Carbohydrates:** 7g / **Protein:** 30g / **Fat:** 11g / **Saturated Fat:** 3g **Fiber:** 2g / **Sugar:** 3g

- 1 lb. of chicken thighs (boneless, skinless)
- 1 teaspoon of paprika
- ½ teaspoon garlic powder
- ¾ teaspoon of onion powder
- ¼ teaspoon of cayenne pepper or to taste
- ¼ teaspoon of thyme
- ¼ teaspoon of oregano
- 1 teaspoon of salt
- ½ teaspoon of pepper divided
- 2 cloves of garlic (minced)
- 3 bay leaves
- ½ white diced onion
- 1 celery stalk (chopped)
- 1 green bell pepper (diced)
- 2 teaspoons of chicken-stock (concentrate) or 1 teaspoon of chicken-bouillon granules (reduced-sodium)
- ½ cup of diced tomatoes
- 2 teaspoons of Worcestershire sauce
- ½ lb. sliced andouille sausage
- 1 lb. of jumbo shrimp (peeled and deveined)
- 20 oz. of frozen riced-cauliflower
- Green onion (chopped), optional
- Hot-sauce, optional

Instructions:

1. At the bottom of the Slow-Cooker, put the chicken thighs.
2. Combine the paprika, powdered garlic, onion powder, thyme, oregano, cayenne, pepper, and salt in a small bowl. Sprinkle over the chicken half of this combination.
3. Garlic cloves, chopped onion, bay leaves, chopped celery, concentrated chicken stock, diced tomatoes, chopped green pepper, Worcestershire sauce, and sliced andouille sausages are all added to the chicken.
4. Cook for 6 hours on low (or 3 hours on high).
5. Remove the cover after 5 hours (or 2 ½ if cooked high) and stir the jambalaya, cutting the chicken into pieces while you stir. It should be soft to make it easy to shred. Add the cauliflower rice, shrimp, and remaining mixture of spices. Return the cover to the crockpot and cook the rest of the time. Serve garnished with hot sauce and chopped green onions.

83. Crockpot Cauliflower Fried Rice

Servings: 4 / **Prep. Time:** 15 min. / **Cook Time:** 4 hrs. 30 min.

Ingredients:

- 2 heads of cauliflower
- 2 tbsp. of ginger-garlic puree (or fresh-garlic and ginger root, peeled and minced)
- ½ cup of vegetable-broth
- 2 eggs
- 1 cup of frozen vegetable-mix
- ½ cup of boars-head turkey-ham (diced) optional
- ¼ cup of green onions (diced)
- ¼ cup of cilantro, optional
- 2 tbsp. of lite (low sodium) soy sauce or just to taste it

Instructions:

1. Cut off the florets of every cauliflower head. Remove the stems. In a big food processor, position the florets. Pulse until it crumbled fine.
2. Add the cauliflower crumbs, vegetable broth, and ginger-garlic puree into a big crockpot. Cover and cook for 2 hours on high, or 3–4 hours on low.
3. Whisk the eggs and scramble them into a skillet 30 min. before eating. To the crockpot, add eggs, diced turkey ham, and frozen veggies. Let it cook for an additional 30 minutes or till the frozen veggies are hot. Stir in the cilantro and green onions. Drizzle to taste with soy sauce.

Calories: 172 / **Total Fat:** 5g / **Saturated Fat:** 2g / **Trans Fat:** 0g / **Cholesterol:** 92mg / **Sodium:** 405mg / **Carbohydrates:** 22g / **Dietary Fiber:** 8g / **Sugars:** 6g / **Protein:** 13g

84. Coconut Curry Chicken with Cauliflower Rice (Keto, low-carb)

Servings: 4–6 / **Prep. Time:** 10 min. / **Cook Time:** 1 hr.

Ingredients:

- 4 large chicken breasts (cut into even cubes)
- 1 teaspoon of kosher salt
- ½ teaspoon of black pepper
- ½ teaspoon of Moroccan-seasoning, optional
- 1 teaspoon of cumin
- ¼ teaspoon of paprika
- 2 teaspoons of turmeric
- 13.5oz can of coconut milk
- 1 teaspoon of lemon juice
- 1 teaspoon of extra virgin olive oil
- 3 garlic cloves (minced)
- 2 teaspoons of ginger, freshly grated
- ¼ cup of yellow-onion (chopped)
- 1.5 tablespoon of butter (salted)
- To taste: Red-Pepper Flakes
- To taste: Fresh-Cilantro

Instructions:

1. Break the chicken in even cubes (about 1/4 "thick).
2. Whisk salt, pepper, cumin, paprika, Moroccan seasoning, and turmeric in a glass bowl, until well blended.
3. Combine lemon juice, olive oil (extra virgin), coconut milk, garlic, onion, and ginger in a separate bowl. Mix well.
4. Combine the two bowls' contents into one, then mix properly.
5. Add the chicken to the bowl to ensure the curry mixture covers it entirely.
6. Cover to permit 2–3 hours of marinating, or overnight.
7. Melt the butter over med-high heat in a pot or wide skillet.
8. Apply the mixture of chicken curry and enable it to bring to a boil.
9. Lower the heat to moderate, cover with a lid and simmer for 50 min.

Calories: 276 / **Total Fat:** 21g / **Cholesterol:** 9mg / **Carbohydrates:** 5g / **Net Carbohydrates:** 4g / **Fiber:** 1g / **Sugar:** 1g / **Protein:** 15g

85. Keto Chicken Gumbo

Servings: 5 / **Prep. Time:** 10 min. / **Cook Time:** 4 hrs.

Ingredients:

- 3 tbsp. of olive-oil
- 1 lb. of chicken thighs (fat and skin-trimmed)
- 8oz of smoked turkey-sausage, (chopped into 1-inch pieces)
- 1 ½ tablespoon of garlic (minced)
- ½ cup of red onion (diced)
- 1 green bell pepper (diced)
- 2 celery stalks (chopped)
- 225g of okra (sliced into pieces)
- 1 ½ tablespoon of cajun-seasoning
- 1 ½ tablespoon of arrowroot-starch
- 4 ½ cups of chicken broth (low sodium)
- 2 bay leaves
- Meal Garnish
- Cauliflower rice

Instructions:

1. On the crockpot, the sauté function is turned on, then add 1 tbsp. of oil and chicken thighs (chopped). Sauté until the thighs are ready for around 6 to 8mins. Toss in the smoked turkey sausage, then remove it. Cook 3 to 5mins. further, then remove.
2. Add the left olive oil, garlic, bell pepper, celery, okra, and red onion to the crockpot and stir continuously to (a) stick nothing; and (b) brown the okra, so no slimy gumbo is made, around 2 to 4 mins.
3. Add the Cajun seasoning and blend to allow the spices to bloom. Add starch arrowroot and mix again. When continuing to stir, gradually add the chicken broth.
4. Fold in the turkey sausage and the chicken. Offer it a stir, lets the toss in Two bay leaves, and carry to simmer.
5. Adjust the setting to slow and cook for 4 hours on med-high heat. Enjoy cauliflower rice raw or cooked to keep it low in carb and satisfying

Calories: 321 / **Protein:** 24g / **Fat:** 21g / **Carbs:** 12g / **Fiber:** 3g / **Sugar:** 3g

86. Low-carb Vegan Rice and Beans

Servings: 6 / **Prep. Time:** 5 min. / **Cook Time:** 4 hrs. 5 min.

Ingredients:

- 2 packages of frozen cauliflower-rice (12 oz./340g each)
- 2 packages of black soybeans drained and rinsed
- 1/2 cup (80g) of hemp seeds
- 1 cup of vegetable-broth/stock
- 3 tbsp. of olive oil
- 3 tbsp. of garlic powder
- 1 tsp. of onion powder
- 1 tsp. of cumin
- 1 tsp. of chili powder
- 1 tsp. of cayenne powder
- 1 tbsp. of Mexican oregano
- Garnishes of choice

Instructions:

1. Add all to the Slow-Cooker except the Mexican oregano and blend as effectively as possible. Let cook for around 3–4 hours on high before the "rice" is soft. Stir the oregano.

2. Garnish and serve as needed.

Calories per serving: 299 / **Fat:** 20.2g / **Carbs:** 4.9g / **Net Protein:** 19.3g / **Fiber:** 11.8g

87. Crockpot Rice Pudding

Servings: 6 / **Prep. Time:** 5 min. / **Cook Time:** 3 hrs. 30 min.

Ingredients:

- 3 eggs, lightly beaten
- ¼ cup of (low-carb) sugar substitute
- 1 tsp. of vanilla extract
- 1 can (13.5 ounces) of coconut cream or coconut milk
- 7 oz. (1 bag) of miracle rice, properly rinsed and dried
- Nutmeg half teaspoon

Instructions:

1. Prepare by rinsing miracle rice in a big bowl of water and then draining. Then, mix in a dry pan to extract excess water, until the rice feels as it's stuck to the pan. Remove the rice pan from the flame.
2. Lightly grease the baking dish 1–½ quart that fits into the Slow-Cooker.
3. Combine eggs, sweetener, coconut cream, and vanilla extract in mixing bowl, and water with the electric mixer till it's combined. You will want to rinse off any of the liquid in coconut cream at the can bottom.
4. Stir the miracle rice into the mixture of cream.
5. Pour the mixture into the ready dish and evenly spread it out. Sprinkle over with nutmeg.
6. On the crock bottom, put an aluminum foil or rack, then pour 2 cups of hot water into it.
7. Cover the baking dish with a foil and put it in a Slow-Cooker rack.
8. Cover and simmer for 3–3 ½ hours on high or until the pudding is ready.
9. Before serving, Chill thoroughly for better results.

Net Carbs: 2.4g / **Serving:** 133g / **Calories:** 180 / **Carbohydrates:** 3.8g / **Protein:** 4.2g / **Fat:** 17.4g / **Saturated Fat:** 14.2g / **Fiber:** 1.4g / **Sugar:** 2.4g

88. Salsa Chicken Cauliflower Rice Bowls

Servings: 4 / **Prep. Time:** 10 min. / **Cook Time:** 6 hrs.

Ingredients:

- 1 pound of chicken-breasts/thighs
- 1 ½ cup of salsa
- 1 tbsp. of oil
- 1 head (about 4 cups) of riced-cauliflower
- ¼ cup of chopped cilantro, divided
- 1 cup of cheddar cheese (shredded)
- 4 ounces of guacamole
- 4 ounces of black olives (sliced)
- Sour cream, for serving

Instructions:

1. Add the chicken and salsa to a Slow-Cooker. Cook for 4 hours on high or on low for 6 hours. Shred into two forks before serving.
2. Heat oil over med-high heat in a large skillet. Stir in the riced cauliflower, then sauté until the cauliflower rice is tender, around 5 minutes. Put in cilantro, stir, switching off the heat.
3. By creating a cauliflower rice base, assemble bowls topped with cheese, guacamole, shredded salsa chicken, black olives, extra cilantro, and sour cream.

Calories: 491 / **Sugar:** 7.5g / **Fat:** 27.7g / **Saturated Fat:** 10.1g / **Carbohydrates:** 23.3g / **Fiber:** 8.6g / **Protein:** 39.9g

89. Keto Chicken and Cauliflower Rice Soup

Servings: 10 / **Prep. Time:** 30 min. / **Cook Time:** 1 hr.

Ingredients:

- 2 ½ pounds of chicken breasts (boneless, skinless)
- 8 tbsp. of butter (1 stick)
- ¼ cup of celery (chopped)
- ½ cup of onion, chopped
- 4 garlic cloves (minced)
- 2 (12 ounces) packages of steamed cauliflower-rice,
- 1 tbsp. of parsley
- 2 tsp. of poultry-seasoning
- ¾ tsp. of rosemary
- 1 tsp. of salt
- ¾ tsp. of pepper
- 4 ounces of cream cheese
- 4 ¾ cups of chicken broth
- 1 ½ cups of heavy cream
- 1/3 cup of cheddar cheese

Instructions:

1. In a Slow-Cooker, put skinless, boneless chicken breasts and cover them with salt, pepper, and water or chicken broth. Cook for 3 hours on high, or 6 hours on low.
2. Shred the chicken that has been cooked and set aside.
3. Melt butter in a tall stockpot, then add the garlic, celery, onions, and sauté over med heat until they appear to become translucent.
4. In the meanwhile, following instructions on the box, pop the steam bags riced
5. Add riced cauliflower and all the spices to the vegetables and stir on med-heat for 7 minutes until that all the herbs and vegetables are blended in.
6. Stir in the cream cheese till melted.
7. Add chicken shredded, heavy cream, and chicken broth and bring to a simmer.
8. Turn the heat down to low as it hits a boil and cook with the lid off for 15 min.
9. Serve

Calories: 415 / **Carbohydrates:** 6g / **Protein:** 27g / **Fat:** 30g / **Fiber:** 1g

90. Slow-Cooker Keto Turkey Kale Rice Soup

Servings: 8 / **Prep. Time:** 15 min. / **Cook Time:** 8 hrs.

Ingredients:

- 1 tbsp. of avocado oil or olive
- ½ cup of shallots (chopped)
- 1 garlic clove (minced)
- ½ cup of carrots (sliced)
- 1 cup of celery (sliced)
- 1 tsp. of salt
- ½ tsp. of pepper
- ½ tsp. of dried basil
- ½ tsp. of dried oregano
- ½ tsp. of dried thyme
- 2 cups of turkey-cooked (chopped)
- 4 cups of turkey-broth/chicken/bone broth
- 4 cups of water
- 1 cup of miracle-rice
- 4 cups of kale-stems removed, (chopped or 100g)
- ¼ cup of parsley-grated parmesan-cheese (fresh, chopped)

Instructions:

1. Heat oil in a wide skillet and cook garlic, carrots, celery, and shallots, frequently stirring for around 10 minutes until vegetables are softened.
2. Add the salt, basil, pepper thyme, and oregano, and cook for another minute.
3. Adding all ingredients to the big crockpot, except the miracle rice.
4. Cook on high for 3–4 hours, until the kale is tender. Rinse the miracle rice well, then add the last 30 min. of cooking time to the pot.
5. Parmesan cheese and fresh parsley on top.

Fat: 4g / **Saturated Fat:** 1g / **Carbohydrates:** 5g / **Fiber:** 1g / **Sugar:** 1g / **Protein:** 8g / **Net Carbs:** 6g

91. Crockpot Luau Pork with Cauli Rice

Servings: 9 / **Prep. Time:** 8 min. / **Cook Time:** 6 hrs. 30 min.

Ingredients:

- 3 lb. of pork-roast (shoulder/butt)
- 4 slices of bacon-hickory smoked and nitrate-free-
- 2 tbsp. of Hawaiian black lava sea salt
- 6 garlic cloves (minced)
- 2 tablespoons of hickory-liquid smoke (optional)
- cauli rice
- 3 cups of cauliflower
- 2 tablespoons of homemade organic or chicken-broth
- ¼ teaspoon of garlic powder
- 1/8 teaspoon sea salt

Instructions:

1. To a high setting, set crockpot, and line the crockpot bottom with the slices of the raw bacon. Sprinkle the top of the bacon with minced garlic.
2. If needed, cut a little fat off the bottom of the roast.
3. Poke and stab holes all around and into the roast with a small knife.
4. In a little pinch bowl, add black lava sea salt (1 ½–2 tbsp.) and use your fingers to rub salt over the roast.
5. Put the roast in the crockpot, fat side down. Over the top of the roast, add liquid smoke and cover the crockpot. Cook for 4 to 6 hours on high, then for 2 hours on low. For 8 hours to 10 hours, it could also cook on low. If the cooking time is over, take a fork to pull out the roast in the crockpot (if finished, it can quickly fall out). In the crockpot, stir the shredded pork and bacon and cover. Cook 30 minutes on low.
6. If you plan to create the cauliflower rice, it's time to start preparing it now. Steam the cauliflower for 20 min. or 5 minutes in the microwave. Place the cauliflower (slightly cooled) and add garlic, sea salt, and chicken broth to the food processor.
7. Process until it shapes the texture of rice.
8. Put a Cauli rice scoop on a plate then add a shredded luau pork scoop.
9. Enjoy.

Calories: 182 / **Carbohydrates:** 2g / **Protein:** 14g / **Fat:** 13g / **Fiber:** 0.9g / **Sugar:** 1g

92. Crock-Pot Asian Beef and Paleo 'Rice' Bowls

Servings: 4 / **Prep. Time:** 10 min. / **Cook Time:** 4 hrs.

Ingredients:

- 2 lb. of grass-fed boneless chuck steak
- ¼ cup of coconut aminos
- 3 tbsp. of coconut-sugar
- 3 garlic cloves (crushed)
- 1 tsp. of toasted sesame oil
- ½ tsp. of ground ginger
- ½ tsp. of fine sea salt
- ¼ tsp. of freshly ground pepper
- Pinch red pepper flakes are optional

Paleo Rice Bowls:

- 1 medium head of cauliflower
- 2 garlic cloves (minced)
- 2 tablespoon of extra-virgin olive oil
- 1 red pepper, sliced
- 1 sliced onion
- 2 cups of broccoli
- Add any vegetables that you desire as it is optional
- ¼ cup of coconut aminos
- 3 tbsp. of rice-vinegar
- ¼ tsp. of red pepper flakes
- ½ tsp. of fine sea salt, just to taste
- 2 scallions (sliced for garnish)
- ½ tsp. of sesame seeds, for garnish

Instructions:

1. Season chuck salt and pepper and sear on both sides for 30 secs. in a wide, greased skillet.
2. In the Slow-Cooker, place chuck steak (boneless).
3. Mix the marinade in a bowl and pour the chuck. Cook 4 hours on high.
4. Remove from the crockpot then shred, discarding fat once done.
5. In a food processor, pulse the cauliflower until pieces formed rice-sized.
6. Heat 1 tablespoon of oil in a saucepan and one garlic clove until fragrant for 30 seconds. Add the cauliflower rice and blend until soft, for 3–5 minutes. Take off heat and put aside.
7. Add 1 tablespoon of oil along with the last clove of garlic to the pan. Add the vegetables and sauté until translucent, for 5–8 minutes. Apply amino coconut, rice vinegar, salt, and red pepper flakes. Mix then let it cook for another 5–8 mins., until tender. Add shredded beef and allow to cook for 5 min.
8. Assemble: add Cauli rice in a bowl and add beef mixture/veggie. Garnish with the scallions and sesame seeds. **Calories:** 631 / **Sugar:** 10g / **Fat:** 31.4g / **Saturated Fat:** 8.5g / **Carbohydrates:** 20g / **Fiber:** 4g / **Protein:** 62g / **Cholesterol:** 136mg

93. Slow-Cooker Chicken and Rice Soup

Servings: 6 / **Prep. Time:** 10 min. / **Cook Time:** 4 hrs.

Ingredients:

- 1 ½ lb. of chicken breast (boneless and skinless)
- 1 small onion (finely chopped)
- 3 carrots (finely chopped)
- 3 ribs of celery (finely chopped)
- 3 cloves of garlic, minced
- 3 sprigs of fresh thyme (or 1 tsp. of dried thyme)
- 2 bay leaves, dried
- ¼ cup of dry white wine, optional
- 6 cups of chicken broth
- ¾ teaspoon of salt
- ¼ teaspoon of freshly ground black pepper
- 1 cup of instant white rice
- 2 tablespoons of finely chopped fresh parsley

Instructions:

1. Combine the carrots, celery, onion, garlic, thyme, bay leaves, parsley, white wine, salt pepper, and broth, at the base of the Slow-Cooker; stir. Add chicken breasts (ensure the liquid covers them).
2. Cover and cook on low for around 4 hours or on high for 2–3 hours, until chicken is tender. Move the chicken to the cutting board and shred the chicken into bite-size bits using 2 forks. Drop the sprigs of thyme and bay leaves.
3. In the Slow-Cooker, mix the instant rice in the soup. Cover and cook for 10–15 min. until soft. Placed the shredded chicken back in the soup. Put some parsley. When needed, sample and season with some more salt and pepper. Serve.

Calories: 219 / **Carbohydrates:** 18g / **Protein:** 27g / **Fat:** 4g / **Saturated Fat:** 1g / **Cholesterol:** 73mg / **Sodium:** 1322mg / **Potassium:** 787mg / **Fiber:** 2g / **Sugar:** 2g / **Vitamin A:** 5350IU / **Vitamin C:** 24mg / **Calcium:** 50mg / **Iron:** 2mg

Chapter Ten
Side Recipes

94. Slow-Cooker Three Cheese Spaghetti Squash

Servings: 6 / **Prep. Time:** 15 min. / **Cook Time:** 4 hrs.

Ingredients:

- 1 large spaghetti (squash)
- ¼ cup f butter
- 2 garlic cloves, minced
- 1 ½ ounce of grated asiago cheese
- 1 ½ ounce of grated parmesan cheese
- 1 teaspoon of salt
- ½ teaspoon of pepper
- ¾ cup of shredded mozzarella
- ¼ cup of basil (chopped and fresh)

Instructions:

1. Cut in half the spaghetti squash. In a broad Slow-Cooker, put them cut-side down and cook for 2–3 hours on high or 4 to 6 hours on low. When it can be squeezed easily, the squash is cooked.
2. Switch the Slow-Cooker off, and the squash is removed. To the Slow-Cooker, add butter and garlic and allow the butter to melt.
3. In the meanwhile, scoop out the spaghetti squash seeds using a large spoon. Discard. Scoop out the flesh of the skin and transfer it back to the crockpot. Add the parmesan, asiago, pepper, and salt and toss all the ingredients together. Spread out uniformly over the Slow-Cooker's bottom.
4. Sprinkle mozzarella and replace the crockpot cover. Let it stay until melted in the warm, Slow-Cooker, another 10 min. or so. Sprinkle and serve with fresh basil.

Net Carbs: 6.42g / **Food energy:** 192Kcal / **Total fat:** 13.98g / **Calories:** 125 / **Carbohydrate:** 7.95g / **Total dietary fiber:** 1.53g / **Protein:** 8.29g

95. Slow-Cooker Pepper Jack Cauliflower

Servings: 6 / **Prep. Time:** 10 min. / **Cook Time:** 3 hrs. 30 min.

Ingredients:

- 1 head of cauliflower (cut into 1inch florets)
- 4 ounces of cream cheese
- ¼ cup of whipping cream
- 2 tablespoons of butter
- 1 teaspoon of salt
- ½ teaspoon pepper
- 4 ounces of pepper jack (shredded)
- 6 slices of bacon (cooked, crisp, and crumbled)

Instructions:

1. Grease a Slow-Cooker (4 to 6 quart) on the inside.
2. Stir in the cauliflower, whipping cream, cream cheese, butter, pepper, and salt. Cook on low heat for three hours.
3. Mix after adding the pepper jack. Keep cooking for another 30mins. to an hour, until the cauliflower is soft.
4. Add crumbled bacon and enjoy.

Food energy: 272Kcal / **Total fat:** 21.29g / **Calories from fat:** 191 / **Carbohydrate:** 6.28 / **Protein per serving:** 10.79g / **Total dietary fiber:** 2.01g

96. Slow-Cooker Lemon-Garlic Asparagus (Low-Carb, Paleo, Whole30)

Servings: 8 / **Prep. Time:** 5 min. / **Cook Time:** 2 hrs.

Ingredients:

- 1 bunch of asparagus (rinsed and trimmed),
- 2 to 4 lemon slices
- 1 cup of water (for pressure cooker)

Sauce:

- ¼ cup of lemon-juice
- ¼ cup of water
- 2 garlic cloves (minced)
- 1 teaspoon of basil
- ½ teaspoon of salt
- ¼ teaspoon of red pepper flakes

Instructions:

1. Mix together the ingredients for the sauce in a bowl.
2. Add asparagus to the Slow-Cooker bottom. Pour over the sauce.
3. Cook 1–2 hours high, 2–4 hours, low. Before serving, top lemon slices.

Calories Per Serving: 75 / **Total Fat:** 2.3g / **Saturated Fat:** 0.6g / **Total Carbohydrate:** 16g / **Dietary Fiber:** 0.8g / **Sugars:** 3.9g / **Protein:** 1.7g

97. Crockpot Buttered Garlic Mushrooms

Prep. Time: 5 min./**Cook Time:** 3 hrs.

Ingredients:

- 2 lb. of whole mushrooms (fresh)
- 1 stick of butter
- 4 garlic cloves (peeled and crushed)
- 1 teaspoon of Italian seasoning
- ½ teaspoon of salt

Instructions:

1. Put the mushrooms in the crockpot.
2. In the oven, heat the butter and blend the crushed garlic, the Italian seasoning, and the salt.
3. To ensure that all mushrooms are coated, stir the garlic butter over the mushrooms and mix well.
4. Put the cover and cook for 3 hours on low.
5. Use a slotted spoon for removing the crockpot mushrooms, then serve with sprinkled fresh parsley.

Calories: 57 / **Carbohydrates:** 11g / **Protein:** 5g / **Fiber:** 1g / **Sugar:** 3g

98. Crockpot Loaded Cauliflower Casserole

Servings: 6 / **Prep. Time:** 10 min. / **Cook Time:** 3 hrs.

Ingredients:

- 24 ounces of frozen cauliflower
- 4 ounces of cream cheese
- 1 cup of mozzarella cheese
- 1 cup of cheddar cheese
- 3 ounces of bits of bacon
- 2–3 green onions (diced)

Instructions:

1. Use a greased crock or a Slow-Cooker lining.
2. In the crock, place half of the cauliflower in just one layer. Add the half of cream cheese on the cauliflower into cubes or strips, then cover. Sprinkle the frozen cauliflower with half of the shredded cheese and bacon pieces. Now add cream cheese, cauliflower layering, and then sprinkle on top with shredded cheese and bacon. Cook for 3 to 4 hours at low. When frying, stir once or twice. Sprinkle on top green onions, and serve.

Calories: 294 / **Carbohydrates:** 11g / **Protein:** 17g / **Fat:** 21g / **Saturated Fat:** 11g / **Fiber:** 4g / **Sugar:** 3g

99. Slow-Cooker Ratatouille

Servings: 8 / **Prep. Time:** 20 min. / **Cook Time:** 4 hrs.

Ingredients:

- 2 tbsp. of coconut oil (or ghee)
- 1 large onion (chopped)
- 6 garlic cloves (minced)
- 1 large eggplant (chopped)
- 1 orange bell pepper (chopped)
- 4 zucchini squash or summer squash
- 1 cup of grape tomatoes (chopped)
- 2 tbsp. of tomato paste
- 1 tsp. of oregano (dried)
- 1 tsp. of ground pepper
- ½–1 tsp. of sea salt
- 1 cup of fresh basil, (chopped)

Instructions:

1. In a big Slow-Cooker, add all the ingredients except basil, cover, and cook. On high, cook for 3–4 hours or on low for 5–6 hours. When the vegetables have softened, the ratatouille is set. If you are concerned that the ratatouille is very watery, remove the crockpot cover for the last hour and cook on high. Gently whisk in the fresh basil just before eating. Serve cold or warm, as a side or over a whole grain like rice or quinoa.

Calories: 127 / **Sugar:** 9g / **Fat:** 5g / **Carbohydrates:** 23g / **Fiber:** 10g / **Protein:** 5g

100. Slow-Cooker Low-Carb Santa Fe Chicken

Servings: 8 / **Prep. Time:** 10 min. / **Cook Time:** 10 hrs.

Ingredients:

- 1 (15 ounces) can of black beans (rinsed and drained)
- 1 (14.5 ounces) can of chicken-broth (fat-free)
- 1 (14.5 ounces) can of diced tomatoes along with green chile peppers
- 1 (8 ounces) bag of corn (frozen)
- ¼ cup of fresh cilantro, chopped
- 3 scallions (chopped)
- 1 tsp. of garlic powder
- 1 tsp. of onion powder
- 1 tsp. of ground cumin
- Cayenne pepper
- 1 pinch of salt
- 1 ½ pound of chicken breast halves (skinless and boneless)

Instructions:

1. In the crockpot, mix black beans, diced tomatoes, chicken broth, green chili peppers, cilantro, scallions, corn, garlic powder, onion powder, cumin, salt, and cayenne pepper. Season with salt the chicken breast and place mixture of the beans on top.
2. Cook for 9 ½ hours on low.
3. Move the chicken from the crockpot to the cutting board; cut it in strands, move it to the crockpot and stir in the mixture of the beans.
4. Continue to cook for 30 more minutes on low.

Calories: 177.8 / **Protein:** 22.5g / **Carbohydrates:** 17.6g / **Fat:** 2.3g

101. Crockpot Chicken Fajitas

Servings: 6 / **Prep. Time:** 10 min. / **Cook Time:** 3 hrs.

Ingredients:

- 1 ½ pound of chicken breasts (boneless, skinless)
- 8 ounces of cream cheese
- ½ cup of prepared salsa (jarred/homemade)
- 1 garlic clove (minced)
- 1 tsp. of paprika
- 1 tsp. of cumin
- 1 tsp. of salt
- ½ tsp. of ground black pepper
- 2 bell peppers (any color)
- 1 onion
- 1 lime (cut into wedges)

Instructions:

1. In a Slow-Cooker (5–6 quart), add the chicken breasts, salsa, garlic, cream cheese, paprika, cumin, pepper, and salt.
2. In strips, slice the onion and bell peppers and add to the crockpot.
3. Cover and cook for 3 hours on high or 6 hours on low, or until the chicken is cooked through and easily shreds.
4. Using two forks, shred the chicken and squeeze out the lime over the fajitas.
5. To blend the mixture, stir well.
6. Spoon the cauliflower rice over the fajitas and top with additional toppings you want, like avocado, sour cream, and cheese.
7. Serve it warm.

Calories: 276 / **Fat:** 17g / **Carbohydrates**: 8g / **Fiber:** 3g / **Protein:** 25g

102. Slow-Cooker Cabbage and Onions

Servings: 12 / **Prep. Time:** 15 min. / **Cook Time:** 6 hrs.

Ingredients:

- ¼ cup of bone broth
- 12 cups (1 large head) of cabbage (chopped/shredded)
- 2 cups of onions (sliced)
- 2 tablespoon of extra-virgin olive oil
- 2 teaspoons of minced garlic
- 2 teaspoon of ground cumin
- 1 teaspoon of ground mustard
- 1 teaspoon of salt
- Pepper half teaspoon

Instructions:

1. In the Slow-Cooker, pour bone broth and add all rest of the ingredients. To mix properly, stir.
2. Cover and cook 5–6 hours or until soft, on low heat.

Net Carbs: 4g / **Calories:** 52 / **Fat:** 2g / **Carbohydrates:** 6g / **Fiber:** 2g / **Sugar:** 3g / **Protein:** 1g

103. Crock-Pot Zucchini and Yellow Squash

Servings: 6 / **Prep. Time:** 5 min. / **Cook Time:** 6 hrs.

Ingredients:

- 2 cups of medium zucchini (sliced and quartered)
- 2 cups of medium yellow squash (sliced and quartered)
- ¼ tsp. of pepper
- 1 tsp. of Italian seasoning
- 1 tsp. of garlic powder
- ½ tsp. of sea salt
- ¼ cup of butter (cut in cubes)
- ¼ cup of parmesan cheese/asiago cheese grated

Instructions:

1. In the crockpot, place the sliced zucchini and the yellow squash.
2. Sprinkle with Italian seasoning, pepper, sea salt, and garlic powder.
3. Top with pieces of butter, cheese, and the rinds of pork.
4. Cover and cook for 4–6 hours on low.

Calories: 122 / **Carbohydrates:** 5.4g / **Protein:** 4.2g / **Fat:** 9.9g / **Fiber:** 1.7g / **Net Carbs:** 3.7g

104. Slow-Cooker Mongolian Beef

Servings: 4 / **Prep. Time:** 10 min. / **Cook Time:** 6 hrs.

Ingredients:

- 1 ½ lbs. of flank/sirloin steak
- 1/3 cup of swerve brown
- ¼ cup of water
- ¼ cup of tamari/soy sauce
- 2 tablespoons of sesame oil
- 2 garlic cloves (minced)
- ½ teaspoon of ground ginger
- ¼ teaspoon of red pepper flakes
- ½ teaspoon of glucomannan powder
- 2 chopped green onions
- Sesame seeds, to be used for sprinkling

Instructions:

1. Slice the beef against the grain, quite thinly. That works better when semi-frozen (not solid rock). Place the meat in a Slow-Cooker bottom.
2. Whisk the brown sugar substitute, tamari, sesame oil, water, garlic, red pepper flakes, and ginger together in a med bowl or glass. Pour over meat.
3. Put the cover on the crockpot and cook for 4–6 hours on low, or for 2 to 3 hours on high.
4. When the beef is cooked, scoop some broth out of the pot in a bowl. Whisk in glucomannan powder until combined, then add back the broth in the pot, then stir to coat.
5. Sprinkle beef with sesame seeds and the sliced green onions and serve over cauliflower rice.

Calories: 417 / **Carbohydrates:** 2g / **Fat:** 25.4g / **Fiber:** 0.4g / **Protein:** 35.7g

105. Slow-Cooker Crack Chicken

Servings: 6 / **Prep. Time:** 10 min. / **Cook Time:** 3 hrs.

Ingredients:

- ½ cup of chicken broth (low sodium)
- 1 tbsp. of ranch seasoning mix
- 4 chicken breasts (boneless and skinless)
- 1 block (8ounces) of cream cheese, at room temperature, (cut up to 4 pieces for easier melting)
- 2 cups of shredded cheddar cheese (divided)
- 6 slices of bacon (chopped)
- For serving chopped green onions
- For garnish: chopped fresh parsley

Instructions:

1. Pour the chicken broth in a Slow-Cooker and whisk in the seasoning mixture of the ranch.
2. Add the chicken breasts to the crockpot and mix in the chicken to coat.
3. Cover with the lid and place for 5 hours on low or 2–3 hours on high.
4. When finished, use two forks to remove the cover and shred the chicken inside the crockpot.
5. Stir in the cream cheese and shredded cheddar cheese (1½ cups); stir until melted and blended.
6. Top with leftover cheddar cheese; cover the lid to allow the melting of the cheese.
7. Remove the cover and sprinkle the top with sliced bacon.
8. Garnish with parsley and green onions.
9. Serve with salads, wraps, burgers, or lettuces cups.

Net Carbs: 4g / **Calories:** 469 / **Fat:** 36g / **Saturated Fat:** 19g / **Carbohydrates:** 4g / **Sugar:** 1g

106. No-Hassle Crockpot Keto Meatloaf

Servings: 6 / **Prep. Time:** 15 min. / **Cook Time:** 6 hrs.

Ingredients:

For the meatloaf:
- 1 ½ pound of ground beef
- 1 large egg
- 1 tablespoon of oregano
- 2 teaspoons of thyme
- 2 teaspoons of rosemary
- 2 teaspoons of basil
- 2 teaspoon of garlic powder
- 1 teaspoon of pepper
- ½ cup of grated parmesan cheese

For the BBQ sauce:
- ½ cup of homemade beef broth
- 3 oz. of tomato paste (organic, no sugar added)
- ½ teaspoon of granulated stevia
- 1 teaspoon of apple cider vinegar
- ½ teaspoon of dijon mustard
- ¼ teaspoon of smoked paprika
- ¼ teaspoon of red pepper flakes
- ¼ teaspoon of chili powder
- 1 teaspoon of onion powder
- 1 teaspoon of garlic powder
- ¼ teaspoon of cumin
- Salt to taste

Instructions:
1. Combine all ingredients in a dish to create the sauce.
2. Refrigerate after covering with plastic wrap.
3. Put all the ingredients in a big bowl to create the meatloaf and blend until well mixed.
4. The mixture is shaped on a large tinfoil sheet, into a loaf.
5. Put the meatloaf in a Slow-Cooker, with the foil.
6. Cover with a cap and cook for 5 hours on low.
7. With 1/3 cup of BBQ sauce, remove the cover and brush the sides and top.
8. Cover then cook for more 30 to 60 minutes.
9. Raise the meatloaf carefully, slice, and serve with the reaming BBQ sauce.

Calories: 242 / **Carbohydrates:** 6.3g / **Fat:** 7.9g / **Sugar:** 5.2g / **Protein:** 30.2g

107. Slow-Cooker Low-Carb Meatloaf Wrapped in Bacon

Servings: 6 / **Prep. Time:** 10 min. / **Cook Time:** 4 hrs.

Ingredients:

- 500g of bacon
- 700g of ground beef
- 1 small onion (chopped)
- 2 garlic cloves minced
- 1 cup of spinach/kale (chopped)
- 1 cup of bell pepper (chopped)
- 50g of flour
- 1 egg
- Pepper and salt

Instructions:

1. Mix all the ingredients of the meatloaf together in a large bowl, except bacon.
2. Lay flat on the counter a parchment paper large sheet. Arrange the bacon in a rectangle to ensure each bit overlaps. Then, in the middle of the bacon, put the meatloaf mixture, and create a meatloaf shape.
3. Cover the bacon edges around the meatloaf, and tuck ends in the meat. This holds in place the bacon. Using parchment paper to transfer the meatloaf to the crockpot, then flip it gently into the crockpot.
4. Top the meatloaf with the green beans, then cover and simmer. Cook for 4–5 hours at high, or 6–8 hours at low. Drain the liquid when done and remove the cover. Crisp bacon by putting the insert of the Slow-Cooker under the broiler/grill for some minutes in the oven.

Calories: 1088 / **Fat:** 92g / **Total Carbohydrates:** 10g / **Fiber:** 3.1g / **Sugar:** 3.5g / **Protein:** 51g

108. Keto Slow-Cooker Buffalo Chicken

Servings: 8 / **Prep. Time:** 5 min. / **Cook Time:** 3 hrs.

Ingredients:

- 2 pounds of chicken breast/thighs (boneless, skinless)
- 1 cup of franks buffalo sauce
- ¼ cup of butter
- 1 tbsp. of brown sugar substitute
- 2 tsp. of smoked-paprika
- 1 tsp. of garlic powder/minced garlic
- Pepper and salt

Instructions:

1. In a Slow-Cooker, mix the chicken, butter, hot sauce, brown sugar substitute, garlic powder, cayenne pepper, and smoked paprika.
2. Season with salt and pepper to taste.
3. Cook 3 to 4 hours on high, or 6 to 8 hours on low.
4. To shred the chicken, use forks.

Calories: 183 / **Carbohydrates:** 2g / **Protein:** 24g / **Fat:** 9g / **Saturated Fat:** 4g / 1103mg / **Potassium:** 435mg / **Fiber:** 1g / **Sugar:** 1g

Chapter Eleven
Beef

109. Chipotle Beef Barbacoa Recipe (Slow-Cooker/Crockpot)

Servings: 9 / **Prep. Time:** 10 min. / **Cook Time:** 4 hrs.

Ingredients:

- 3 lb. of beef brisket/chuck roast
- 1/2 cup of beef broth
- 2 medium chipotle chiles in adobo
- 5 garlic cloves minced
- 2 tbsp. of apple cider vinegar
- 2 tbsp. of lime juice
- 1 tbsp. of dried oregano
- 2 tsp. of cumin
- 2 tsp. of sea salt
- 1 tsp. of black pepper
- 1/2 tsp. of ground cloves (optional)
- 2 bay leaf (whole)

Instructions:

1. Combine the chipotle chilies in adobo sauce, garlic, lime juice, apple cider vinegar, oregano (dried), cumin, black pepper, sea salt, and ground-cloves (all except for the bay leaves and beef). Purée until it's smooth.
2. Put the pieces of beef into the crockpot. Pour the mixture of puree on the top (from the blender). Now add (whole) the bay leaves.
3. Cook on high for 4–6 hrs. or at low for 8–10 hrs., until the beef is soft to fall apart.
4. Remove (whole) bay leaves. Shred the meat (with two knives) then mix in the juices. For 5-10 min, cover and wait for the beef to absorb more flavor. You can use a slotted spoon for serving.

Calories: 242 / **Fat:** 11g / **Total Carbs:** 2g / **Net Carbs:** 1g / **Fiber:** 1g / **Sugar:** 0.3g / **Protein:** 32g

110. Instant Pot (or Slow-Cooker) Low-Carb Southwestern Beef Stew

Servings: 8 / **Prep. Time:** 20 min. / **Cook Time:** 6–8 hrs.

Ingredients:

- 2 lbs. of beef cubes bite-sized
- 4 tsp. of olive oil
- 1 medium onion, chopped small
- 1 medium poblano chile pepper, chopped small
- 1 tbsp. of crushed/minced garlic
- 2 cans of black olives, well-drained
- 1 cup of frozen cauliflower rice
- 1 (14 oz.) can of beef broth
- 1 cup of salsa
- 1 tbsp. of ground cumin
- 1 tsp. of Mexican oregano
- 1 (14.5 oz.) can of crushed tomatoes
- 2 tbsp. of lime juice

Instructions:

1. Put the Beef-broth (14 oz.) in a saucepan (small one) on the burner and simmer to make it ¾ cups.
2. Chop up the poblano chile, onions, and make garlic. Heat 2 teaspoons of oil in a frying pan and sauté the poblanos and onions for around 3 min. Add garlic, then cook for another 1 min, now add these ingredients to the crockpot.
3. After browning the beef, now add the spices, salsa, and tomatoes (crushed) along with the beef stock (3/4 cup) to the frying pan and simmer. Now add that mixture along with the olives and cauliflower rice to the crockpot.
4. Cook for 6–8 hours on low. You can cook for 3–4 hrs. on high.
5. Mix in the lime juice and serve.

Calories: 468 / **Total Fat:** 31g / **Saturated Fat:** 10g / **Carbohydrates:** 9.6g / **Fiber:** 4g / **Sugar:** 5g / **Protein:** 36g

111. Low-carb Beef Stroganoff

Servings: 4 / **Prep. Time:** 15 min. / **Cook Time:** 6 hrs.

Ingredients:

- 1 brown onion, sliced and quartered
- 2 garlic cloves, crushed
- 2 streaky bacon slices, diced
- 500g of stewing steak beef cubed
- 1 tsp. of smoked paprika
- 3 tbsp. of tomato paste
- 250ml of beef stock
- 250g of mushrooms quartered

Instructions:

1. In the crockpot, place all ingredients.
2. Mix well.
3. Set 6–8 hrs. on low or 4–6 hrs. on high.
4. Optional: you can serve with sour cream.

Serving: 1 / **Calories:** 317 / **Total Carbs:** 8g / **Protein:** 29g / **Fat:** 19g / **Fiber:** 1g / **Sugar:** 4g / **Net carbs:** 7g

112. Slow-Cooker Low-carb Meatloaf Recipe

Servings: 8 / **Prep. Time:** 10 min. / **Cook Time:** 3 hrs.

Ingredients:

- Spritzer bottle Olive oil/cooking spray olive oil
- 2 lbs. of ground sirloin/ground bison
- 2 large eggs
- 1 grated zucchini, squeezed out excess liquid
- ½ cup of parmesan cheese freshly grated
- ½ cup of finely chopped fresh parsley
- 2 garlic cloves, minced
- 3 tablespoons of balsamic vinegar
- 1 tablespoon of dried oregano
- 2 tablespoons of dry onion (minced), or onion powder
- ½ teaspoon of sea salt/kosher salt
- ½ teaspoon of ground black pepper

Instructions:

1. Line a large crockpot with strips of aluminum foil. With non-stick cooking spray or olive oil, spray the foil.
2. Add all the ingredients except cooking spray and the coating ingredients in a large blending bowl. The mixture would be wet/loose.
3. Move the mixture carefully to the crockpot and form into an oblong formed loaf, positioning it on top of the strips of aluminum foil. Put the cover on the crockpot.
4. Cook for 3 hrs. on high, or 6 hrs. on low. Stop providing heat for 15min. until cooking time finishes and unplug the crockpot. Spread ketchup on the top of the Meatloaf and remove the lid. Over the layer of ketchup, place the cheese. Let the meatloaf stay for around 5–10 min., or until the cheese is melted.
5. To take out the loaf from the crockpot, remove the cover, keep each strip end in each palm, and raise it carefully. Move the loaf to a serving plate and with fresh-parsley garnish it. Enjoy it!

Calories: 320 / **Calories Fat:** 20g / **Saturated Fat:** 8g / **Carbohydrates:** 4g / **Fiber:** 1g / **Sugar:** 2g / **Protein:** 26g

113. Barbecue Meatloaf Slow-Cooker

Servings: 10 / **Prep. Time:** 10 min. / **Cook Time:** 6 hrs.

Ingredients:

- 2 lbs. of ground beef lean
- 1 lb. of ground pork lean
- ½ cup of onion chopped
- ½ cup of almond flour
- 1 tsp. of pepper
- 1 tsp. of garlic powder
- 2 large eggs
- 1 tsp. of salt
- 1 cup of easy BBQ sauce sugar-free

Instructions:

1. Mix the ground-beef, onion, almond-flour, ground-pork, salt, garlic powder, and pepper in a large bowl. Add the eggs and blend well with your hands until thoroughly blended.
2. Shaping mixture into a loaf approximately 5 x 9 inches on a wide sheet of tinfoil. Raise the sides of the foil and place it in a crockpot (6-quart).
3. Set the crockpot on low and cook for 5–6 hrs. Brush the top and the sides with almost 1/3 cup of BBQ sauce in the last ½ hr. of cooking.
4. Take the meatloaf out of the crockpot into a serving platter using two serving forks. Slice it and with the rest of the BBQ sauce.

Total Net Carbs: 3.51g / **Food energy:** 369 / **Saturated fatty acids:** 8.73g / **Total fat:** 22.49g / **Calories from fat:** 202 / **Carbohydrate:** 4.95g / **Total Dietary Fiber:** 1.46g / **Protein:** 26.95g

114. Perfectly Simple and Sliceable Crockpot Roast Beef

Servings: 2 / **Prep. Time:** 15 min. / **Cook Time:** 1 hr. 35 min.

Ingredients:

- 2–3 pounds of beef roast
- 2 teaspoons of kosher salt
- 1 teaspoon of black pepper freshly ground
- 2 tablespoons of olive oil

Instructions:

1. Heat the oil over medium heat in a pan. With pepper and salt, season the roast generously. In the hot pan, sear the meat for about 3–4 min on each side until meat is browned. Sear the sides also the roast's top and bottom. Extract from the skillet and put it in the Slow-Cooker. Install an oven-safe meat thermometer into the roast's center and put the cover over the crockpot.
2. Cook the roast at low till the temperature is 140°C. It only took 90 min. to make the roast. It might take twice as long for you, depending on the temperature of the house and how much heat is provided to the Slow-Cooker while cooking.
3. Using meat forks/strong-tongs, transfer the roast to a cutting board and tent it. Before slicing it thin against the grain of the meat, let the beef sit for 20 min. Enjoy.

Calories: 235 / **Protein:** 21g / **Fat:** 16g / **Saturated Fat:** 6g / **Cholesterol:** 78mg

115. Healthified Moroccan Beef

Servings: 8 / **Prep. Time:** 10 min. / **Cook Time:** 10 hrs.

Ingredients:

- 1/2 cup of sliced onion
- 2 lb. of roast beef grass-fed
- 2–4 tbs. of garam masala spices
- 1 tsp. of Celtic sea salt

Instructions:

1. Cut the onion in thin strips, place it in a crockpot. Put the roasted beef over the onions in a cooker. Apply salt and spices. Cook for 8 hrs. at low heat. Shred using a fork and cook the spices to infuse the beef for another two hours at the low setting. Serve over a cauliflower-rice, miracle rice, or a healthified tortilla. Makes eight servings.

Calories: 209 / **Fat:** 9.5g / **Protein:** 30.4g / **Carbs:** 0.7g / **Fiber:** 0 / **Effective Carbs:** 0.7

Chapter Twelve
Chicken

116. Slow-Cooker Mandarin Chicken – Low-Carb and Gluten-Free

Servings: 6 / **Prep. Time:** 10 min. / **Cook Time:** 6–7 hrs.

Ingredients:

For the chicken:
- 6 chicken thighs
- 1 tbsp. of Chinese five-spice powder
- ½ tsp. of kosher salt

For the sauce:
- 1 cup of mandarin orange slices no sugar added
- 1 tsp. of minced garlic
- 1 tbsp. of minced ginger
- 1/2 tsp. of sliced red chilis
- 1 tbsp. of lime juice
- 1 tbsp. of granulated sugar substitute
- 1 tsp. of sesame oil
- 2 tbsp. of fish sauce

Instructions:

1. Rub the salt and five-spice powder on the chicken thighs. Sear the side of the skin down for around 3 minutes on high. Three minutes to turn and sear its other side. In the Slow-Cooker, put the chicken skin side up. In a small cup, add the sauce ingredients (not the xanthan gum) and mix. Pour the chicken in the crockpot. Cook for 4 hours on high, or 6 hours on low. Move the chicken to a serving platter from the Slow-Cooker. Pour in a magic bullet or mixer the remaining sauce and add xanthan gum (1/2 tsp.). For about 20 secs, blend. Pour the chicken onto the platter and then serve soft. Optional is cilantro garnish.

Calories: 392 / **Fat:** 23g / **Net Carbs:** 3.5g / **Protein:** 37g

117. Crock-Pot Slow-Cooker Crack Chicken

Servings: 10 / **Prep. Time:** 10 min. / **Cook Time:** 3 hrs. 10 min.

Ingredients:

- 2 lb. of chicken breast
- 1 tbsp. of dried parsley
- 1 tbsp. of dried dill
- 1 tbsp. of dried chives
- 1 tsp. of garlic powder
- 1 tsp. of onion powder
- ½ tsp. of black pepper
- 16 oz. of cream cheese
- 1 cup of cheddar cheese
- ½ cup of bacon bits (cooked)
- 1/3 cup of green onions (chopped)

Instructions:

1. Add chicken breasts in a single layer on the Slow-Cooker.
2. Sprinkle all the spices and herbs over the chicken.
3. Set cream cheese bits uniformly over the chicken.
4. Cook the chicken on high for 3–4 hours or at low for 6–8 hours, until the chicken is simple to shred.
5. To mix with cream cheese, shred the chicken and stir.
6. Put the shredded cheddar, green onions, and bacon bits together.

Calories: 346 / **Fat:** 23g / **Total Carbs:** 6g / **Net Carbs:** 5g / **Fiber:** 1g / **Sugar:** 1g / **Protein:** 24g

118. Low-carb Spicy Chicken

Servings: 4 / **Prep. Time:** 10 min. / **Cook Time**: 5 hrs.

Ingredients:

- 1 medium onion, chopped
- ½ cup of green/red bell peppers, chopped
- 1/3 cup of water
- 1 tablespoon of vegetable oil
- 1 teaspoon of salt
- 1 teaspoon of garlic powder
- ½ teaspoon of chili powder
- ½ teaspoon of paprika
- ½ teaspoon of Italian seasoning
- ¼ teaspoon of ground ginger
- ¼ teaspoon of black pepper
- 4 chicken breast boneless skinless

Instructions:

1. In the crockpot, mix the onion, water, oil, bell pepper, salt, paprika garlic powder, ground ginger, Italian seasoning, and black pepper. To blend the spices, whisk well.
2. Add the cubes of chicken and stir to coat correctly.
3. Cover and simmer the crockpot for 5 hours on low.
4. Serve warm.

Calories: 183 / **Fat:** 5g / **Carbs:** 5g / **Protein:** 28g

119. Slow-Cooker Low-carb Sesame Ginger Chicken

Servings: 6 / **Prep. Time:** 10 min. / **Cook Time:** 4 hrs.

Ingredients:

- 1 lb. of chicken breast boneless skinless
- 1 lb. of chicken thighs boneless skinless
- ¼ cup of soy sauce low sodium
- ¼ cup of chicken broth low sodium
- 2 packets of stevia (or to taste)
- 2 tbsp. of orange juice
- 2 tbsp. of hoisin sauce
- 2 garlic cloves minced
- 2 tbsp. of fresh minced ginger
- 2 tbsp. of sesame seeds

Instructions:

1. Add chicken to the crockpot.
2. Mix the chicken broth, soy sauce, stevia, hoisin sauce, orange juice, ginger, and garlic.
3. Cook 3–4 hours on high, till the chicken is thoroughly cooked. shred or slice
4. Optional: Do you like a more thick sauce? Add sauce to a little pot from the Slow-Cooker. Just get it to a boil. In the meantime, add 1 tbsp. of cornstarch into cold water. Add and mix well into the boiling sauce. Bring to a boil and cook, stirring continuously before the sauce thickens for 1–2 minutes.
5. Want crispy? Spread chicken on a foil-covered baking sheet and broil it for 3–4 mins. or until crispy.
6. Sesame seeds topping.

Calories: 207 / **Total Fat:** 5g / **Total Carbohydrate:** 5g / **Dietary Fiber:** 1g / **Sugars:** 2g / **Protein:** 32g

120. Low-carb BBQ Chicken in the Slow-Cooker

Servings: 6 / **Prep. Time:** 20 min. / **Cook Time:** 4–5 hrs.

Ingredients:

- 1 clove of garlic, crushed
- 2 tablespoons of golden monk fruit
- 5 tablespoons of tomato paste
- 2 teaspoon of chili powder
- 2 teaspoons of smoked paprika powder
- 3/4 cup of water
- 1 tablespoon of Worcestershire sauce
- 1 teaspoon of onion powder
- 3 tablespoons of butter
- 1 teaspoon of dried mustard
- 4 chicken breasts, skinless
- 6 boneless, skinless chicken thighs
- Pepper and salt

Instructions:

1. Season the chicken liberally on both sides with salt and pepper.
2. Add to the crockpot and cook till the chicken is soft but not falling apart, for 3–4 hours on high or on low.
3. Put the ingredients of the BBQ sauce in a small pan while the chicken is frying, and whisk to mix. Simmer for ten min., then take off.
4. Use foil to line a baking sheet and then spray using cooking spray.
5. Place the chicken on the cookie sheet and brush with BBQ sauce on both sides.
6. Put for five mins. under the broiler, then turn over and broil for another 5 min.
7. Serve with additional BBQ sauce to dip in if needed.

Calories: 37 / **Fat:** 3.3g / **Carbs:** 3.1g / **Fiber:** 0.4g / **Protein:** 0.3g / **Net Carbs:** 2.7g

121. Crockpot Pepper Chicken (Slow-Cooker)

Servings: 4 / **Prep. Time:** 5 min. / **Cook Time:** 6 hrs.

Ingredients:

Place in Crock-Pot right away:

- 3 boneless, skinless chicken breasts
- 1 cup of chicken stock
- 1 tsp. of mustard seeds
- 1 tsp. of garlic powder or 1 crushed garlic clove

Sautee 30 minutes before the chicken is done cooking:

- 1 medium onion, peeled and diced
- 2 bell peppers in thin strips
- 1-2 tbsp. of olive oil
- salt and pepper
- ¼ cup of garlic sweet sauce/Teriyaki sauce

Instructions:

1. Place on the crockpot bottom the chicken breasts. On top, pour the chicken stock. Add the mustard seeds and powdered garlic. Set the timer to six hours and set "high" temperature. Throughout the cooking, switch the breasts around two times, doing for the first 3 hours of the cooking process.
2. Sauté the onions in a pan with 1–2 tbsp. of oil, till slightly golden, about 20 mins. until the chicken is done.
3. Add bell pepper strips and sauté a few more before the pepper takes on a particular color and becomes soft.
4. Shred it with two forks until the chicken is Prepared. Don't remove the remaining liquid but leaving it will help in keeping the chicken moist.
5. Add the sauce you like (Teriyaki sauce/garlic sweet sauce) and sautéed onion and pepper. Season with black pepper freshly ground, sriracha and salt.
6. On a toasted bun.
7. Serve hot.

Calories: 249 / **Fat:** 7g / **Saturated Fat:** 1g / **Carbohydrates:** 13g / **Fiber:** 1g / **Sugar:** 9g / **Protein:** 30g

122. Creamy Chicken with Bacon and Cheese Slow-Cooker (Low-Carb and Keto)

Servings: 8 / **Prep. Time:** 15 min. / **Cook Time:** 3 hrs.

Ingredients:

- 2 lbs. of chicken breasts, boneless skinless
- 3 tablespoons of butter
- ½ tsp. of poultry seasoning
- ½ tsp. of rosemary
- ¼ tsp. of thyme
- 1 tsp. of garlic
- 1/3 cup of chicken broth
- 3 pieces of cooked bacon, crumbled
- 1/3 cup of heavy whipping cream
- 3 oz. of cream cheese
- 1 3/4 cup of cheese
- 3 slices of bacon crumbled
- Salt/pepper

Instructions:

1. Add chicken to Slow-Cooker and next six ingredients.
2. Crumble on top of chicken with cooked bacon (3 pieces).
3. Cook for 6 hours on low or 3 to 3 1/2 on high.
4. Add heavy cream to the Slow-Cooker.
5. Top Dollop cream cheese, stir to mix all the ingredients.
6. Shred chicken in the crockpot, using 2 forks.
7. Put 1 3/4 cups of cheddar cheese, then crumble 3 bits of fried bacon on top.
8. Put the top back onto the crockpot and melt the cheese.

Calories: 408 / **Carbohydrates:** 2g / **Protein:** 33g / **Fat:** 29g / **Saturated Fat:** 15g / **Fiber:** 1g / **Sugar:** 1g

123. Slow-Cooker Chicken Caprese Casserole (Low-Carb, Keto)

Servings: 4 / **Prep. Time:** 10 min. / **Cook Time:** 3 hrs.

Ingredients:

- 2 lbs. of boneless and skinless chicken breasts, cut in 1" cubes
- 28 ounces of diced tomatoes
- 2 cups (approximately 1 bunch) of fresh basil
- 2 cups of shredded mozzarella cheese

Sauce:

- ¼ cup of olive oil extra-virgin
- 2 ½ tbsp. of balsamic vinegar
- ½ tsp. of salt
- 1/8 tsp. of pepper

Instructions:

1. Add to Slow-Cooker chicken, basil, and diced tomatoes.
2. Mix sauce ingredients in a tiny bowl. In the Slow-Cooker, pour sauce. To blend properly, stir.
3. Cook high for 2–3 or low for 4–6 hours.
4. Add the cheese and then cook for another 10–20 min. or till the cheese melts.

Calories Per Serving: 376 / **Total Fat:** 27.5g / **Saturated Fat:** 9.5g / **Total Carbohydrate:** 13.7g / **Dietary Fiber:** 2.8g / **Sugars:** 7.7g / **Protein:** 21.1g

Chapter Thirteen
Pork

124. Crockpot Cola Pulled Pork (Low-carb)

Servings: 10 / **Prep. Time:** 5 min. / **Cook Time:** 8 hrs.

Ingredients:

- 1 tablespoon of butter, melted
- ½ cup of finely chopped onion
- ½ tbsp. of minced garlic
- 1 ¼ cups of coke zero
- 3/4 cup of tomato paste
- ½ cup of water
- 1 tablespoon of Worcestershire sauce
- 3 tablespoons of mustard
- 1 teaspoon of cajun seasoning
- 1 teaspoon of liquid smoke
- ½ teaspoon of paprika
- 1 tablespoon of cumin
- ½ teaspoon of pepper
- 5 lb. of pork shoulder roast
- Salt

Instructions:

1. Put the pork in a Slow-Cooker (6 quarts) and sauté well.
2. In a sauce, combine the remaining ingredients and pour them on top.
3. Cook on low for 8–10 hrs., or until super tender.
4. **Optional Step:** Extract meat and cook sauce, stirring until it reduces to a thick sauce.
5. With two forks, shred, and serve with sauce or juices.

Calories: 244 / **Carbohydrates:** 6g / **Protein:** 28g / **Fat:** 11g / **Saturated Fat:** 4g / **Fiber:** 1g / **Sugar:** 3g / **Net Carbs:** 5g

125. Keto Slow-Cooker Pulled Pork

Servings: 8 / **Prep. Time:** 10 min. / **Cook Time:** 8 hrs.

Ingredients:

- 800g of shoulder/butt pork roast
- 1 tbsp. of tomato paste
- 1 tsp. of ground cumin
- 1 tsp. of paprika
- 1 tsp. of salt
- 1 tsp. of pepper
- 1 tbsp. of onion powder
- 1 tbsp. of garlic powder
- 1 tbsp. of coconut aminos
- 60ml of apple cider vinegar

Instructions:

1. Mix all the seasonings, tomato paste, and coconut amino together in a little bowl.
2. In the Slow-Cooker, put the pork roast, skin side down, then smother the roast entirely with the seasoning paste.
3. Flip the roast until the side of the skin faces up. In the Slow-Cooker, add vinegar by pouring to the side, not over the roast.
4. Place the Slow-Cooker lid on top. Cook the roast on low for 10–12 hours or on high for 8–9 hours.
5. Shred the roast until finished and put the meat back in the juice for 10–15 mins. to relax. The pulled pork absorbs the juice's flavors. Serve, and have fun.

Calories: 181 / **Total Carbohydrates:** 0.1g / **Protein:** 24.7g / **Fat:** 8.3g / **Fiber:** 0.05g / **Sugar:** 0.1g / 9mg / **Net carbs:** 0.1g

126. Low-carb Pork Chops in Crockpot With Spice Rub (Recipe)

Servings: 8 / **Prep. Time:** 5 min. / **Cook Time:** 6 hrs.

Ingredients:

- 1 tbsp. of rosemary dried
- 1 tbsp. of thyme dried
- 1 tbsp. of curry powder dried
- 1 tbsp. of fresh chives chopped
- 1 tbsp. of fennel seeds
- 1 tbsp. of ground cumin
- 1 tsp. of salt
- 4 tbsp. of olive oil
- 2 pounds of pork chops

Instructions:

1. Mix rosemary, curry powder, thyme, chives, cumin, salt, fennel seeds, and ½ olive oil in a bowl.
2. To equally coat the meat, rub pork chops with a spice mix.
3. Load the remainder of the olive oil in the crockpot. In a Slow-Cooker, add the beef, cover, and cook on high for 4 hours, 6 hours on med, or on low for 8 hours.

Calories: 247 / **Carbohydrates**: 1g / **Protein:** 24g / **Fat:** 15g / **Saturated Fat:** 3g / **Cholesterol:** 75mg

127. Low-carb Slow-Cooker Spicy Pulled Pork

Servings: 8 / **Prep. Time:** 5 min. / **Cook Time:** 8 hrs.

Ingredients:

- 3 lbs. of lean pork tenderloin
- 1 onion, quartered
- 4 garlic cloves, sliced
- 4 jalapenos, whole
- 1 tbsp. of paprika
- 1 tbsp. of garlic powder
- 1 tbsp. of chili powder
- 2 tsp. of salt
- 2 tsp. of cumin
- 1 tsp. of pepper
- 1 cup of BBQ sauce (no sugar added or low sugar)
- ½ cup of chicken broth low sodium

Instructions:

1. Mix all the spices and rub the pork tenderloin. In a Slow-Cooker, add the garlic, onions, and entire jalapenos. On top, place the pork.
2. Mix the barbecue sauce and the broth chicken. Pour over pork.
3. Cook for 8 hours on low. Shred with two forks and let the pork rest 30 minutes in sauce with the crockpot open and on low heat for thickening of the sauce.

Calories: 240 / **Total Fat:** 4g / **Saturated Fat:** 1g / **Total Carbohydrate:** 9g / **Dietary Fiber:** 2g / **Sugars:** 6g / **Protein:** 37g

128. Keto Slow-Cooker Pork Roast

Servings: 8 / **Prep. Time:** 10 min. / **Cook Time:** 7 hrs.

Ingredients:

- 4–5 lbs. of pork butt
- 1 tablespoon of garlic powder
- 1 tsp. of Italian seasoning
- 1 teaspoon of dried mustard
- 1 teaspoon of onion powder
- ½ butter stick
- 1 ½ cup of chicken broth/veggie broth
- 1 tsp. of salt
- ½ tsp. of pepper
- Freshly chopped parsley

Instructions:

1. Pepper and salt pork roast liberally.
2. Melt ½ a stick of butter in a hot skillet and sear the roast on every side.
3. To a Slow-Cooker, add pork roast and the remaining butter and pieces from the skillet bottom.
4. Add the other ingredients and cook slowly for 9–10 hours or 6–7 hours on high, or until the roast falls apart.
5. Then shred with two forks and add back to the Slow-Cooker on high for 30 min. to an hour. It would therefore tenderize it by making it rest in its juices.
6. Serve with finely sliced parsley.

Calories: 307 / **Carbohydrates:** 1g / **Protein:** 43g / **Fat:** 13g / **Saturated Fat:** 5g / **Fiber:** 1g / **Sugar:** 1g

129. Keto Cuban Pork (Lechón)

Servings: 20 / **Prep. Time:** 10 min. / **Cook Time:** 8 hrs.

Ingredients:

- 4 pounds of pork shoulder
- 1 tablespoon of dried oregano
- 1 tablespoon of ground cumin
- 1 tablespoon of paprika
- 1 teaspoon of black pepper
- 3 teaspoons of sea salt
- ½ teaspoon of cayenne pepper flakes
- 2 onions, coarsely chopped
- 8 finely minced garlic cloves
- ½ cup of sour orange juice
- ¼ cup of white wine ½ cup of or white vinegar
- 2 bay leaves

Instructions:

1. Blend the salt, sour orange juice, oregano, white wine vinegar, cumin powder, pepper flakes, and garlic in a med bowl. Marinade the pork. Put the pork, along with the bay leaf and onions, within the Slow-Cooker. Cover and let simmer for 8 hours on low heat at least.
2. Drain the meat until the pork is fork-tender, then put it under a broiler on a cookie sheet until the meat crisps.
3. For up to 5 days, refrigerate leftovers or freeze for up to 6 weeks.

Calories: 273 / **Total Fat:** 19.4g / **Saturated Fat:** 7.2g / **Carbohydrates:** 0.8g / **Fiber:** 0.1g / **Sugar:** 0.2 / **Protein:** 21.2g

Conclusion

It seems like many various diet strategies are on the market these days, each promising a new approach to restrict the calories in an attempt to lose weight. The explanation of why all these diets struggle is because the incorrect problem is being addressed.

The amount of calories you eat per day is no concern. It's the form of calories you ingest that cause weight loss challenges. You should go for "Ketogenic crockpot recipes for Quick Weight Loss and Smart Healthier Living" if you're searching for a solution to losing the weight off. The Ketogenic diet (Slow-Cooker) is the right approach that reduces weight more quickly than those of any other plan there and improves your fitness. During the keto diet, you get to eat with comfort and experience some of the best recipes and finest ingredients. Slow-Cookers are perfect because your stuff is essentially dumped in and overlooked until the serving time. Use the crockpot if you realize you're going to come home late but have flexibility in the morning (or sometimes in the evening). Crockpots are a fantastic way to turn cheap meat cuts into satisfying, easy meals. Simple is this 'set and forget' cooking. Try to be organized, so you're not too much in this position. Preparing food for the week or a couple of days at a time would be a great benefit. Take out time for cooking each evening, or once a week for batch cooking.

Printed in Great Britain
by Amazon